DANGEROUS PATIENTS

To Phil
with best wishes

Ronnie

Other titles in the
Forensic Psychotherapy Monograph Series

DANGEROUS PATIENTS

A Psychodynamic Approach
to Risk Assessment and Management

Edited by

Ronald Doctor

Editorial Assistance by

Sarah Nettleton

Foreword by

Pamela Taylor

Forensic Psychotherapy Monograph Series

Series Editor
Brett Kahr

Honorary Consultant
Estela Welldon

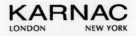

LONDON   NEW YORK

First published in 2003 by
H. Karnac (Books) Ltd.
6 Pembroke Buildings, London NW10 6RE

British Library Cataloguing in Publication Data

A C.I.P. for this book is available from the British Library

ISBN: 1-85575-297-2

10 9 8 7 6 5 4 3 2 1

Edited, designed, and produced by Communication Crafts

Printed in Great Britain

www.karnacbooks.com

CONTENTS

SERIES FOREWORD

Brett Kahr

School of Psychotherapy and Counselling,
Regent's College, London
and
The Winnicott Clinic of Psychotherapy, London

Throughout most of human history, our ancestors have done rather poorly when dealing with acts of violence. To cite but one of many shocking examples, let us perhaps recall a case from 1801, of an English boy aged only 13, who was executed by hanging on the gallows at Tyburn. What was his crime? It seems that he had been condemned to die for having stolen a spoon (Westwick, 1940).

In most cases, our predecessors have either *ignored* murderousness and aggression, as in the case of Graeco–Roman infanticide, which occurred so regularly in the ancient world that it acquired an almost normative status (deMause, 1974; Kahr, 1994); or they have *punished* murderousness and destruction with retaliatory sadism, a form of unconscious identification with the aggressor. Any history of criminology will readily reveal the cruel punishments inflicted upon prisoners throughout the ages, ranging from beatings and stockades, to more severe forms of torture, culminating in eviscerations, beheadings, or lynchings.

Only during the last one hundred years have we begun to develop the capacity to respond more intelligently and more humanely to acts of dangerousness and destruction. Since the advent of psychoanalysis and psychoanalytic psychotherapy, we now have access to a much deeper understanding both of the aetiology of aggressive acts and of their treatment; and nowadays we need no longer ignore criminals or abuse them—instead, we can provide compassion and containment, as well as conduct research that can help to prevent future acts of violence.

The modern discipline of forensic psychotherapy, which can be defined, quite simply, as the use of psychoanalytically orientated "talking therapy" to treat violent, offender patients, stems directly from the work of Sigmund Freud. Almost one hundred years ago, at a meeting of the Vienna Psycho-Analytical Society, held on 6 February 1907, Sigmund Freud anticipated the clarion call of contemporary forensic psychotherapists when he bemoaned the often horrible treatment of mentally ill offenders, in a discussion on the psychology of vagrancy. According to Otto Rank, Freud's secretary at the time, the founder of psychoanalysis expressed his sorrow at the "nonsensical treatment of these people in prisons" (quoted in Nunberg & Federn, 1962, p. 108).

Many of the early psychoanalysts preoccupied themselves with forensic topics. Hanns Sachs, himself a trained lawyer, and Marie Bonaparte, the French princess who wrote about the cruelty of war, each spoke fiercely against capital punishment. Sachs, one of the first members of Freud's secret committee, regarded the death penalty for offenders as an example of group sadism (Moellenhoff, 1966). Bonaparte, who had studied various murderers throughout her career, had actually lobbied politicians in America to free the convicted killer Caryl Chessman, during his sentence on Death Row at the California State Prison in San Quentin, albeit unsuccessfully (Bertin, 1982).

Some years later, Melanie Klein concluded her first book, the landmark text *Die Psychoanalyse des Kindes* [*The Psycho-Analysis of Children*], with resounding passion about the problem of violence in our culture. Mrs Klein noted that acts of criminality invariably stem from disturbances in childhood, and that if young people could receive access to psychoanalytic treatment at any early age, then much cruelty could be prevented in later years. Klein expressed the hope that: "If every child who shows disturbances that are at all severe were to be analysed in good time, a great number of these people who later end up in prisons or lunatic asylums, or who go completely to pieces, would be saved from such a fate and be able to develop a normal life" (1932, p. 374).

Shortly after the publication of Klein's transformative book, Atwell Westwick, a Judge of the Superior Court of Santa Barbara, California, published a little-known though highly inspiring article, "Criminology and Psychoanalysis" (1940), in the *Psychoanalytic Quarterly*. Westwick may well be the first judge to commit himself in print to the value of psychoanalysis in the study of criminality, arguing that punishment of the forensic patient remains, in fact, a sheer waste of time. With foresight, Judge Westwick queried, "Can we not, in our well nigh hopeless and overwhelming struggle with the problems of delinquency and crime, profit by medical experience with the problems of health and disease? Will we not, eventually, terminate the senseless policy of sitting idly by until misbehavior occurs, often with irreparable damage, then dumping the delinquent into the juvenile court or reformatory and dumping the criminal into prison?" (p. 281). Westwick noted that we should, instead, train judges, probation officers, social workers, as well as teachers and parents, in the precepts of psychoanalysis, in order to arrive at a more sensitive, non-punitive understanding of the nature of criminality. He opined: "When we shall have succeeded in committing society to such a program, when we see it launched definitely upon the venture, as in time it surely will be—then shall we have erected an appropriate memorial to Sigmund Freud" (p. 281).

In more recent years, the field of forensic psychotherapy has become increasingly well constellated. Building upon the pioneering contributions of such psychoanalysts and psychotherapists as Edward Glover, Grace Pailthorpe, Melitta Schmideberg, and more recently Murray Cox, Mervin Glasser, Ismond Rosen, Estela Welldon, and others too numerous to mention, forensic psychotherapy has now become an increasingly formalized discipline that can be dated to the inauguration of the International Association for Forensic Psychotherapy and to the first annual conference, held at St. Bartholomew's Hospital in London in 1991. The profession now boasts a more robust foundation, with training courses developing in the United Kingdom and beyond. Since the inauguration of the Diploma in Forensic Psychotherapy (and subsequently the Diploma in Forensic Psychotherapeutic Studies), under the auspices of the British Postgraduate Medical Federation of the University of London in association with the Portman Clinic, students can now seek further instruction in the psychodynamic treatment of patients who act out in a dangerous and illegal manner.

The volumes in this series of books will aim to provide both practical advice and theoretical stimulation for introductory students and for senior practitioners alike. In the Karnac Books Forensic Psychotherapy Monograph Series, we will endeavour to produce a regular stream of high-quality titles, written by leading members of the profession, who will share their expertise in a concise and practice-orientated fashion. We trust that such a collection of books will help to consolidate the knowledge and experience that we have already acquired and will also provide new directions for the upcoming decades of the new century. In this way, we shall hope to plant the seeds for a more rigorous, sturdy, and wide-reaching profession of forensic psychotherapy.

As the new millennium begins to unfold, we now have an opportunity for psychotherapeutically orientated forensic mental health professionals to work in close conjunction with child psychologists and with infant mental health specialists so that the problems of violence can be tackled both preventatively and retrospectively. With the growth of the field of forensic psychotherapy, we at last have reason to be hopeful that serious criminality can be forestalled and perhaps, one day, even eradicated.

References

Bertin, C. (1982). *La Dernière Bonaparte*. Paris: Librairie Académique Perrin.

deMause, L. (1974). The evolution of childhood. In: Lloyd deMause (Ed.), *The History of Childhood* (pp. 1–73). New York: Psychohistory Press.

Kahr, B. (1994). The historical foundations of ritual abuse: an excavation of ancient infanticide. In: Valerie Sinason (Ed.), *Treating Survivors of Satanist Abuse* (pp. 45–56). London: Routledge.

Klein, M. (1932). *The Psycho-Analysis of Children*, trans. Alix Strachey. London: Hogarth Press and The Institute of Psycho-Analysis. [First published as *Die Psychoanalyse des Kindes*. Vienna: Internationaler Psychoanalytischer Verlag.]

Moellenhoff, F. (1966). Hanns Sachs, 1881–1947: the creative unconscious. In: F. Alexander, S. Eisenstein, & M. Grotjahn (Eds.), *Psychoanalytic Pioneers* (pp. 180–199). New York: Basic Books.

Nunberg, H., & Federn, E. (Eds.) (1962). *Minutes of the Vienna Psychoanalytic Society. Volume I: 1906–1908*, trans. Margarethe Nunberg. New York: International Universities Press.

Westwick, A. (1940). Criminology and Psychoanalysis. *Psychoanalytic Quarterly*, 9: 269–282.

EDITORS AND CONTRIBUTORS

KRISTIAN ALEMAN is a psycohologist and psychoanalyst in private practice in Stockholm, Sweden, and a member of the Swedish Psychoanalytical Association. He is doing his doctoral thesis on a psychoanalytic perspective of personality assessment and drug addiction, differentiating between psychotic and non-psychotic drug abusers.

DANIEL ANTEBI is a consultant general psychiatrist currently working in inner-city Bristol, with responsibility for ethnic minorities. He did his higher training in Nottingham and research into the psychological contribution to seizures at Burden Neurological Hospital, Bristol. He completed the Foundation Course in Psychoanalytical Psychotherapy at the Tavistock Clinic and South Trent Training Scheme, Nottingham. He has been involved in management and service development for the past five years.

RONALD DOCTOR is a consultant psychiatrist in psychotherapy and a college tutor at the West London Mental Health NHS Trust. He trained at the Tavistock and Portman NHS Trust and is a member of the British Psychoanalytical Society. He was formerly a visiting psychiatrist at HM Wormwood Scrubs Prison and supervisor and external examiner for the Forensic Psychotherapy Course at the Portman Clinic. He is on the executive board of the International Association for Forensic Psychotherapy.

MARY BROWNESCOMBE HELLER is a consultant clinical psychologist who has worked in the NHS for over twenty years. She completed her training at the Tavistock Clinic in 1993 and subsequently became a member of the British Psychoanalytical Society. She currently manages a psychoanalytic psychotherapy service in the NHS based in Middlesborough, Teesside, and is on the training committee of the North of England Association for Training in Psychoanalytic Psychotherapy. She is completing her doctoral thesis on the relationship between childhood experience of loss and trauma and chronic post-traumatic stress disorder in adulthood.

JOHN LOWE is consultant psychiatrist to the psychiatric intensive care unit and the crisis resolution team at St Charles Hospital. He trained at the Maudsley Hospital and the Institute of Group Analysis, and his research interest is the importance of the therapeutic alliance in mental health work. He has a special interest in general hospital liaison psychiatry and social systems.

RICHARD LUCAS is a consultant psychiatrist at St Ann's Hospital and a member of the British Psychoanalytical Society. He is Founding Chairman of the General Psychiatry Section of the Association for Psychoanalytical Psychotherapy in the NHS. He has a particular interest in the integration of analytic concepts within general psychiatry, and he has written on many related subjects, including the psychotic wavelength, puerperal psychosis, cyclical psychosis, and the life and legacy of R. D. Laing.

CARINE MINNE is a consultant psychiatrist in forensic psychotherapy at Broadmoor Hospital and the Portman Clinic. She is a member of the British Psychoanalytical Society. She specializes in the application of psychoanalysis to the treatment of forensic psychiatric patients, and she has a particular interest in the provision of long-term continuity of psychotherapy, as patients move through different levels of security.

SARAH NETTLETON is a psychoanalytic psychotherapist working in private practice and at the West Middlesex University Hospital. She is a member of the British Association of Psychotherapists and is on the editorial board of the *BAP Journal*.

PAMELA TAYLOR is Professor, Special Hospital Psychiatry, at the Institute of Psychiatry, King's College, London, and Honorary Consultant Psychiatrist, Broadmoor Hospital, and the South London and Maudsley Trust. Her main research interests include the nature of relationships between psychosis and violence, treatment of personality disorder, and long-term outcomes for offender patients. She is a co-editor and author of four books: *Forensic Psychiatry, Clinical Legal and Ethical Issues; Violence in Society; Couples in Care and Custody;* and the forthcoming *Treatment of Personality Disorder*.

IAN TREASADEN is a consultant forensic psychiatrist at The Three Bridges Medium Secure Unit and honorary senior lecturer in forensic psychiatry at Imperial College School of Medicine. He trained in forensic psychiatry in Southampton, at the Maudsley and Bethlem Hospitals in London, and at Broadmoor Hospital. His research interests have focused on patients in medium-secure units, and he is co-author of *Textbook of Psychiatry*.

ESTELA V. WELLDON is honorary consultant psychiatrist at the Portman Clinic. She is the founder and ex-director of the Diploma Course in Forensic Psychotherapeutic Studies at University College London, honorary founder and Honorary President for Life of the International Association for Psychotherapy, and an honorary member of the Institute of Group Analysis. She is the author of *Mother, Madonna, Whore: The Idealisation and Denigration of Motherhood* (1997).

FOREWORD

Pamela J. Taylor

Since it has been known that there is a significant—if only slightly increased—risk of violence among people with some of the more serious mental disorders (e.g. Taylor & Estroff, 2003), views that formal "tools" for assessment of risk should be adopted in such populations have been gaining ground (e.g. Maden, 2003). These "tools" are psychological assessment schedules generally derived from statistical analyses of data collected by various means from broadly relevant samples of people. The analyses are used to draw out those personal characteristics that distinguish people who are violent from those who are not. Some of these scales have been used in attempts to predict violence. Some appear to be good at distinguishing between groups in which many people will be violent and groups in which few will be violent. The usual task that faces clinicians, however, is one of assessing an individual, achieving a result that will inform a treatment and management strategy for restoring or maintaining safety, then implementing that strategy.

The individualization of assessment and management inevitably means some deviation from standardized schedules and, more often, the substitution or the addition of "clinical judgement".

Proper concerns have been raised about this, because the process of clinical judgement is often not transparent, or it may be poorly recorded or communicated. A number of research publications have reported better group predictions with the use of standardized risk-assessment schedules (actuarial tools) than "clinical judgement", but even they, while they define the parameters of the tools, never offer definitions of this clinical judgement. It is all the more confusing when different results follow such comparisons as different statistical analyses are applied to the same data (Gardner, Lidz, Mulvey, & Shaw, 1996; Lidz, Mulvey, & Gardner, 1993). Part of the problem is that clinical judgement is an immensely complex process and, hence, difficult to present with the sort of consistent standards achievable using actuarial tools. If they achieve nothing else, the production of decision trees through iterative analysis of social and clinical data (e.g., Monahan et al., 2000) has provided an illustration of this difficulty, given the wealth of data collection and elaborate mathematical treatment of it necessary to produce quite short branches. Just as those people who are working with standardized instruments of assessment are now striving to make their tools more relevant to the real clinical world, with the incorporation of more clinical and dynamic elements, so people who, essentially, use their own person as their main assessment tool must facilitate improved scrutiny of how that works. They must also provide clear guidance on standards and replicability of the techniques and take a lead in their evaluation. This book provides an important basis for doing that.

It seems obvious that, as interpersonal violence is, by definition, an interaction between two or more people, its evaluation can only be completed by assessment within relationships in which one party, at least, has been professionally trained, or is being professionally supervised, or both. However, researchers in the field, who are increasingly without clinical experience, do not always recognize this. One of the most valuable aspects of the book is the way in which it illustrates, often with powerful clinical examples, not only how such relationships may be used to enhance risk assessment and management, but also how easy it is for that process to be perverted. Critics of the clinical narrative formulation would perhaps tend to emphasize the latter—and, indeed, it is regularly a matter of concern to many of us who are not psychodynamically trained how, without such training, we can maintain both sufficient caring for engagement with a patient to take place *and* the full necessary objective powers to maintain accuracy and high quality in the work of the recognition of pathology and its interpretation. In the practice of forensic psychiatry, many of us turn to psychodynamically trained psychotherapists to assist with standard setting and, in effect, personal audit. Others remain suspicious of the psychodynamic approach, because conventional quantitative research techniques for evaluation have played so little part in its evolution. Furthermore, with its lengthy and highly specialist training, it is sometimes viewed as touching too closely on a heady mixture of faith and freemasonry to be relevant. This book should help to dispel such suspicions and encourage more people to draw on the discipline to reduce the frequency and seriousness of violence in the context of mental disorder.

Nevertheless, while acknowledging that there may be unique elements in the circumstances of anyone who has committed an act of serious antisocial violence, and that depth of understanding is unlikely to be achieved in large epidemiological samples, single retrospectively reported case histories will not in themselves fill the gaps left by grand statistical design. Those reporting in this way might disproportionately select outstanding cases or unusual episodes from the course of treatment—it is these that stick in the mind—or, perhaps, even their successes. Thus, it is helpful to see the discipline in such reporting. Clear statements of how a case came to be selected for such attention are important. It is also crucial to know how elements in the assessment, the assessor, the assessed, and the resultant treatment or management fitted in with evidence-based approaches and thus adhered to a recognizable standard, as well as how they deviated from these, and thus perhaps break new ground or emphasize the power of individual difference. There is clearly an important place for an approach that interprets evidence-based practice as following not only from the body of research-based evidence but also from the evidence of the individual's person and circumstances. It may be regarded as unfortunate that the retiring editor of the *British Journal of Psychiatry* saw fit to abolish case reports as merely "psychiatric trivia" (Wilkinson, 2003), but I fear that in practice they often have been, and the discipline advocated by the *British Medical Journal* in providing evidence-based case reports is rarely achieved. At their best, psychotherapeutic assessments go a long way towards achieving this. Indeed, one of the things that most attracted me to psychodynamic psychotherapy as a process useful in this field was the capacity of some my colleagues thus trained to formulate clinical hypotheses about behaviour patterns of concern, which they would then test in the transference.

Developments are now occurring within the field of dynamic psychotherapy that will enable more standardization in the presentation of assessment data, without, I think, loss of the valued depth that the process ordinarily brings—this is an exciting way forward that is emerging as this book comes to publication. Operational Psychodynamic Diagnostics (OPD: OPD Task Force, 2001) allows presentation of the data elicited in assessment along five axes: one a rather conventional clinical axis that maps onto the International Classification of Diseases (WHO, 1992), but the others picking up the richness of experience of illness and readiness for treatment, interpersonal relationships, conflicts, and defence structures. How wonderful it is to see science and clinical skills merging in this sort of way in the service of patients and, ultimately, of all of us in society.

So, read on. We will not achieve safety for our patients or for those others whom a few of them may threaten until all those working in the psychodynamic psychotherapies can adopt a scientific rigour in evaluating the effects of their work. Equally, we will not achieve such safety until the added value of this special approach in providing detailed and specialist knowledge of individuals and their interactions is widely recognized. This book is a valuable addition to achieving a truly balanced and holistic approach, and I feel privileged to have been asked to write a few words of introduction for it.

DANGEROUS PATIENTS

Introduction

Ronald Doctor

This book brings together clinicians who specialize in various aspects of forensic psychiatry and psychotherapy in order to consider the difficult and problematic issue of risk assessment. The prediction of violence is notoriously unreliable, and it offers a particular challenge to mental health workers because it involves real danger. It has come to be recognized by a number of researchers (Buchanan & Leese, 2001; Dolan & Doyle, 2000; Farnham & James, 2001; Mullen, 1999) that the actuarial model of risk assessment based on epidemiology has failed. This predictive approach is seen here as a defence against coming into real contact with violent patients. It will be proposed that we should return instead to the depth and breadth of the clinical experience itself, entering into the inner world of the patients and their object relationships, meeting and facing the feelings as they emerge within the microcosm of the transference and the countertransference. This approach provides a unique opportunity for therapist and patient to discover and explore the violence, both conscious and unconscious, within a safe environment.

However, this is a demanding option, which involves risk on various levels. Of course, workers do not want to get physically hurt, but there are also emotional risks. Being in the presence of a violent patient induces enormous anxiety, and our thinking may become impaired. There is a danger that our own emotional violence when faced with a violent patient may threaten to undermine both our self-esteem and our sense of professional identity.

The chapters in this volume represent a variety of contributions to a psychodynamic understanding of danger and risk. The book begins with a general survey of current psychodynamic approaches to these issues within mental health settings, including hospital outpatient departments, psychiatric wards, and medium- and high-security hospitals—all places in which violence is a stock-in-trade. When dealing with patients who pose a risk to themselves and to others, accurate assessment of risk and dangerousness is vital for the safety and protection of all those involved.

There is also an exploration of the importance of the psychoanalytically orientated assessment consultation. This represents a critical moment of choice for both patient and therapist. Within the harmonies and discords, the false starts, and the emerging themes of the initial encounter is to be found, in essence, much of what is to come during the course of the treatment.

Countertransference is an inevitable part of all patient contact. In its broadest sense it means the worker's emotional response, which stems both from the specific relationship with the particular patient and from the character and disposition of the worker. Conscious countertransference can usually be controlled and may shed useful light on aspects of the patient's personality and ways of relating. However, when the countertransference is unconscious, it may give rise to well-rationalized but destructive acting out by the carer. When faced with a difficult and potentially dangerous patient, our instinct is to protect ourselves by retreating emotionally into what Hinshelwood calls a "scientific attitude" (1999). Typically, this reaction is given an objective justification, but there is a real danger that this objectification can then blind us to aspects of what is happening subjectively, both in the patient and in ourselves. This depersonalization may be invited and encouraged by the psychotic patient's removal from the world of ordinary human rapport. Conversely, the patient with a severe personality disorder offers a relationship, but one that is too intensely suffused with human feelings that are usually very unpleasant. These patients make us feel manipulated, as though we are impelled to conform to a pattern of relating that they are imposing: we feel provoked and persecuted, and we can become rejecting, hostile, and abusive. We all carry a desire within ourselves for an all-embracing answer that will allow us to avoid facing indescribably difficult psychotic states of mind, and we need to monitor ourselves constantly in order to ensure that we are not falling for some seductively welcome rationalization. Patients in dangerous, psychotic states of mind will tend to deny and explain away their own behaviour, and this can lead to a serious underrating by the assessor of the true level of risk.

When viewed from a psychoanalytic perspective, even the most apparently insane violence has a meaning in the internal world of the person who commits it. There is a need to understand this meaning and to learn from it, in the attempt to prevent further violence. One of the objectives of this publication is to provide the professional working in this area with a means of approaching the subject with enriched understanding, in the hope that the risks of violence in their patients may be reduced.

Each contributor has emphasized that reliable assessment of risk is primarily based on the ability to perceive and to bear the unbearable psychic pain and on an awareness of the complex defensive manoeuvres used to avoid reality. Failure to understand the unconscious communications of the patient can lead to faulty or inadequate risk assessment and, thereby, to situations in which violence may escalate.

Daniel Antebi's chapter introduces the concept of risk assessment in a psychiatric setting, focusing on the fundamental conflicts and anxieties of practitioners who have to assess risk as part of their daily experience. He draws a distinction between actuarial and clinical assessment and discusses their relative importance in individual cases. He describes "risk pathways", exploring the way in which seemingly trivial decisions along these pathways can contribute to the overall risk outcome. He discusses the importance of containment in enabling more freedom and flexibility in risk management, and he suggests that the patient's experience of being contained in itself produces a safer clinical and analytical space within which to work.

Ian Treasaden's chapter deals with risk assessment in the medium-secure unit. In contrast to the other contributions, he describes the standard psychiatric approach to the assessment and management of risk and concentrates on the day-to-day practice of risk assessment with dangerous patients.

Richard Lucas's chapter, written from the perspective of a psychiatrist and psychoanalyst working in general psychiatry, proposes that risk assessment should be focused at the individual clinical level, with each patient being considered as unique. He considers the importance of clinically relevant frameworks of understanding when faced with disturbing and potentially unpredictable acting-out behaviour. He describes how these frameworks, founded on psychoanalytic insights, help to reduce the danger inherent in patients' psychotic states of mind and provide containment for the staff's anxieties, encouraging realistic recognition of their human limitations.

John Lowe, in his chapter on the psychodynamic assessment of violence in the general medical hospital, offers a number of clinical vignettes from the medical ward. He describes characteristic medical scenarios in which patients act as agents or mediators of violence, usually against their own bodies. This is often, though not always, with the aim of attacking either the minds and capacities of their carers or their own non-bodily functions. Characteristically, the carer's reaction is based on an organized, albeit unconscious, misunderstanding that arises out of a need not to "see" what the patient is attempting, also unconsciously, to communicate. This failure to "see" may play into the symptomatic structure of the patient's disturbance, leading to a repetition or even an escalation of the violent acting out.

Carine Minne's chapter deals with psychoanalytic aspects of risk containment in the high-security hospital. She concentrates on the very dangerous patient and describes the case of a man who has committed an apparently motiveless murder. She suggests that regardless of their diagnosis, patients who have carried out serious violent offences demonstrate a high degree of unawareness, and that this seems to the patients to be necessary for their psychic survival. She considers that the task of the forensic psychotherapist is the cultivation of awareness in the patient's mind.

Mary Brownescombe Heller's chapter considers the concept of projective identification as a form of communication. People may place in others aspects of themselves (feelings, experiences, thoughts) that they cannot bear to recognize as belonging in their own internal worlds. She emphasizes that with the borderline patient it is very important to understand one's countertransference in order to make a proper assessment of the risk of violence.

Estela Welldon's chapter focuses on her countertransference while assessing a mother's parenting abilities. She describes the unbearable psychic pain she felt when confronted with a mother who really loved her baby and believed that she was the one who should be the carer, but who simultaneously knew she was incapable of doing so.

Ronald Doctor's chapter considers violence as an aspect of perversion. He discusses Glasser's concept of the core complex and presents the clinical example of a patient who used cross-dressing as a perverse solution to outbursts of uncontrollable aggression.

Kristian Aleman's chapter describes psychotherapy with a patient suffering from a destructive narcissistic personality disorder and dependence on stimulant-type drugs. He suggests that the patient's manifest sexual behaviour was both a defence against envy and, at the same time, an attack on the envied object.

Note

Throughout this volume, for the sake of simplicity, in nonspecific cases we have used the feminine pronoun for clinicians and the masculine pronoun for patients.

CHAPTER ONE

Pathways of risk:
the past, the present,
and the unconscious

Daniel Antebi

Implicit within any construct of risk is the fact that it can be only partially predictive. This means that sometimes, no matter how thorough the risk-assessment and risk-management process, events will occur either because they were unpredictable or because the risk-assessment process produces a false negative result. Moreover, the more sophisticated and accurate the predictive abilities of risk assessment become, the rarer and, therefore, the more catastrophic will any incident appear to those who are not directly involved.

Much of the work and research around risk assessment focuses on trying to conceptualize risk, profiling the typical perpetrator of violence, or on managing risk factors in the acutely disturbed patient (Duggan, 1997). For general psychiatrists, assessing and dealing with the potential risk of violence to themselves or to others is a daily anxiety-provoking experience. Each new patient who enters the consulting-room brings with him the unknown, and this stress may be experienced by the clinician several times a day. The idea of risk is one with which practitioners have an highly ambivalent relationship, as it raises fundamental conflicts and anxieties. There is the moral and social conflict between one's role as a crime prevention officer and the way in which that role may or may not conflict with the role of psychiatrist and confidante. There are the anxieties associated with the possible overt and direct risks to oneself, one's family, and other members of staff. Lastly, there is the potential of a serious incident to cause damage not only to one's sense of self, but also to one's sense of judgement and, ultimately, to one's reputation. All this means that the practitioner will inevitably bring some internal dissonance both to the conceptualization of risk and to the consultation with the patient. The clinician must therefore have the personal ability and the appropriate environment in which to try to contain such conflict and anxiety, as inability to do so will inevitably be perceived by the patient, and the risks inherent in the consultation will increase.

In this chapter I should like to review some of the factors that are commonly accepted to have some predictive value in violent acts, many of which are well rehearsed in the literature, and to understand them in the context of the patient's history and the clinical presentation, through both conscious and unconscious communication. From the point of view of the general psychiatrist, this requires the ability to consider simultaneously both actuarial and clinical information, and to assess their relative importance in each individual case.

Risk is often described in terms of an event outcome, such as the likelihood of a violent act, but there are numerous risk-influencing decisions that need to be taken by the clinician before this end point—for example, managing the risk of disengagement or clarifying the options if treatment fails. Such factors all have an impact on the process of risk assessment as the patient moves through a pathway of care. I also explore, therefore, risk pathways and how seemingly trivial decisions along these pathways contribute to the overall risk outcome. Numerous enquiries report a string of minor systematic mistakes or failures culminating in a catastrophic event.

Finally, I address the issue of containment, both for individual clinicians and for organizations. Risk can only be managed safely if the containment of clinician anxieties is seen as a priority, both by the clinicians themselves and by the organization. The creation of such an environment enables more freedom and flexibility in risk taking and in itself reduces risk and produces a safer clinical or analytic space within which to work.

There are two main conceptual approaches to the consideration of risk assessment—the actuarial or mathematical and the clinical (Buchanan, 1999). The actuarial involves the collection of facts about the patient, including demographic data, history (specifically previous episodes of violence), and current presentation. These facts are then weighted according to some formula and a figure is arrived at, which apparently gives a predictive value to the likelihood of a future act of violence. The problem with such an approach is that many of the "facts" that should be part of this process are not really facts but actually individual clinical judgements. For instance, how does one grade or rate the presence, severity, and content of a delusion? Does it make a difference whether such a delusion is part of a systematized set of delusional beliefs? How systematized does it have to be? It is unlikely that such psychopathology is quantifiable except in very crude terms.

The clinical approach, on the other hand, is seen as informal and not amenable to quantitative assessment, and it leaves the power with the clinicians. Taking a clinical approach results in an assessment that is very difficult to quantify because of the absence of any external validation. Consequently, employing organizations such as health trusts or social-work agencies are unable to manage risk in a coherent and auditable manner and therefore cannot take meaningful medico–legal responsibility for the actions of their clinicians. For this reason, a model for risk assessment and management must take into account the reality that each clinical situation is unique. Alongside this is the need for a formal structure that is understandable and repeatable.

The past

Pattern recognition forms the essence of good and containing clinical practice. It is the basis for the assessment, the diagnosis, and the treatment of all patients, whatever mind/brain model is employed by the clinician. The biologist will understand psychopathology in terms of structural abnormalities in the brain or neurotransmitter dysfunction. It is assumed that these abnormalities are persistent or recurrent and will therefore present in repeatable symptom clusters the detail of which will be patient-specific. The recurrence of these particular symptom clusters and their material relationships within the brain provide the basis for a biological model. The cognitive behaviourist will recognize patterns in terms of antecedents or stimuli, behaviour and consequences, or as repeated cognitive distortions. Again analyses of sequences of behaviours or thoughts are identified by their repeatable patterns. The social theorist will argue that given a particular social or political environment, there will be an understandable and inevitable psychological reaction from those who are subject to it. The psychoanalyst comes to recognize repeated patterns of unconscious behaviour and their relationship to the patient's conscious world. This will be understood in terms of defences such as projection and splitting. All these models are underpinned by the fact that there are recognizable patterns to people's behaviour, and this gives us the possibility of making some predictions about future behaviour. The truism "the best predictor of the future is the past" clearly has some basis in clinical reality. It also has a strong basis in a formal or informal actuarial approach. The fact that it is fundamentally a statistical model means that it gives an indication of who is the high-risk patient or which is the high-risk situation.

This historical pattern can, however, only form a context in which the present can be understood and contained. The model takes particular events and predicts that, because a particular event happened once in a particular context, this event is more likely to happen again. If it happens more than once, it is *very* likely to happen again. In terms of predicting actual human behaviours, however, it fails, because it can never predict a particular act at a particular time. The ability to make more detailed predictions about the timing of an act depends on being able to listen to and understand the conscious and unconscious communication of the patient in the present. The importance of the historical context is that it helps to make sense of the present.

Certain factors and patterns in the patient's history are important when considering risk. Clearly a past history of violence of any sort must be taken seriously, especially when the patient minimizes the importance of that violence. One must also explore the meaning, quality, and consequences of the violent act. The ability of the patient to offer an understanding (whether psychotic or otherwise) gives the clinician an indication as to whether there was some degree of psychological containment in his actions or whether the act was an impulse with little or no cognitive correlate. The quality may be sadistic or frenzied and will give an indication of the mental state of the perpetrator at the time of the attack. For instance, an attack resulting in are multiple stab wounds is more likely to happen where the relationship between perpetrator and victim is close. The behaviour after the event gives an indication of the degree of remorse on the part of the patient.

From a phenomenological perspective, a history of psychosis and, more particularly, congruity between the delusional beliefs or hallucinations and the act are always significant. For some patients whose psyche may be very fragmented, behaviour can be unpredictable and unconnected to expressed internal experience. On the other hand, a patient with a paranoid psychosis can sanely murder his mother in order to inherit her money. Particular attention should always be paid to a history of command hallucinations (Junginger, 1995). Direct instructions to the patient, particularly if they have been violent in content, may precede acts of violence. Diagnostically, patients who have multiple diagnoses or co-morbidity and who are perceived as "difficult to engage" often suffer from psychotic illness, have chaotic lifestyles, and frequently misuse alcohol and drugs. This combination—particularly the effects and sequelae of intoxication with drugs or alcohol—is highly unpredictable and for many patients violence can be intoxication-dependent. A particular psychotic disorder that is relevant is morbid jealousy or Othello syndrome (Shepherd, 1961) in which one party is convinced that their partner is having an affair. This belief is based on delusional thinking—that is, the evidence for coming to such a belief is based on a misinterpretation of events and therefore does not preclude the partner actually having an affair. A history of morbid jealousy must always be identified with an high risk of violence and may ultimately involve such measures as the breaking of confidence on the part of the clinician.

Non-psychotic indicators of violence occurring in the context of relationship difficulties are associated with patterns of enmeshment, jealousy, or separations. These are important, as such dynamics are likely to be repeated in the transference and to create potential risk to the clinician. Other diagnoses associated with increased likelihood of violence are psychopathy and the disinhibition associated with head injury. The use of particular prescribed drugs such as benzodiazepines can also lead to violent disinhibition. Gathering such detailed information lends itself to hypothesizing the nature of the patient's internal world and patterns of behaviour. Such hypotheses can be monitored, tested, and modified as the relationship with the patient develops. One should also bear in mind that the only approach an enquiry panel can take after an incident is to assess and evaluate the history as taken to consider whether enough attention was paid to particular facts and whether the information was recorded and passed to the relevant people. The stuff of serious incident enquiries is often about previous episodes not being taken sufficiently seriously, warnings not being heeded or information not being shared appropriately (Reed, 1997).

Having collated the above information, it is therefore crucial that it is recorded and organized in an understandable format. There are, however, clinical dangers in having well-documented notes and a formal risk-assessment process within an organization. It means that an environment is created wherein both the organization and the individual clinician, having labelled a patient as "high risk", can abrogate responsibility and avoid anxiety. With the future enquiry at the back of our minds, we want to claim that we did all we could and went through the accepted procedure. The patient is split off as bad, and we may cease the struggle to understand and to help. We can avoid the risk and danger to ourselves, our reputations, and our own internal worlds by being the good crime prevention officer. The outcome is a patient who is damned both in the clinicians' own mind and in the minds of the agencies trying to manage him. The hope we should bring to each clinical situation is lost and that will inevitably be experienced by the patient. The consequence of this is an *increase* in dangerousness. This is not to say that all adverse events are preventable but we must be careful to use historical risk assessment not as a tool of persecution but, rather, as an aid to achievable containment.

The present

Using the above historical information as a background, the presentation of the patient at each consultation can be understood within that context. The presenting risk can be assessed along two axes: (1) the content of the communication and presenting symptoms, and (2) the diagnostic formulation. The overt content of the communication is relatively straightforward. Direct and specific threats against an individual, either rationally or psychotically driven, are always significant. One should enquire about the extent of prior planning to the act—for instance, has a weapon been acquired? What efforts are to be made to avoid detection? Often if homicide is contemplated, there is the intention to commit suicide afterwards. Patients may make vague and non-specific threats about what they may do to a third party. Such threats must be fully explored and assessed with a knowledge of whether the patient has previously committed acts of violence and in the context of some understanding of the personality, including the ability to control impulse. Increasingly violent or sexual fantasies should also be considered as possible precursors to an act of violence, including sexual violence. Again, such symptoms must be carefully and fully explored. The importance of the presence of paranoid delusions and command hallucinations, as discussed above, should alert the clinician to further exploration of violent fantasies. Areas that the patient hints at or avoids discussing may also be relevant. That which is not said is often more important than that which is. After the first assessment, an initial diagnostic formulation is made. In terms of risk, this should contain an assessment of personality with some emphasis placed on impulse control, misuse of psychoactive substances, and the presence of delusional thinking.

The unconscious

Assessment of unconscious processes that may alert the clinician to risk requires some overall understanding of the patient's psychodynamics and personality structure. It is often suggested that the clinical hunch is unscientific as it is unquantifiable and often beyond description. However, such experiences should be acknowledged as important by clinicians. "Hairs on the back of the neck" or "gut feelings" may be somatic projections that are communications emerging from within the patient's unconscious. The fact that they are somatic suggests that the patient has no contact with them as they are very primitive experiences. On a slightly more sophisticated level, being with the patient may induce an intense feeling of fear that is not reflected in the conscious communication. This lack of congruence between the conscious and unconscious suggests a splitting off of the experience of fear leaving the patient with a sense of omnipotence. This clearly has the potential to be a source of risk.

Such projections must be explored either internally by the therapist or, if possible, with the patient, and thought through in the context of the patient's personality. If being with a patient whom you know to have strong borderline elements to their personality and who has poor impulse control engenders a feeling of intense anxiety or fear, it is essential that each communication is carefully considered and that the clinician makes adequate personal preparations for the next meeting. Projections inevitably stimulate a countertransference response in the assessor. Time taken to distinguish between and reflect on these inner experiences will provide some containment in the assessment and some objectivity to the real risks.

Other projections that may alert the clinician are the feeling of being toyed with by the patient, which may suggest a sadistic element to the personality or that the patient experiences some triumph in making the clinician or services fail. This suggests the possibility of a destructive impulse as a part of the personality or defensive structure. There are particular experiences—namely coldness or emptiness—that clinicians should note. When these are experienced in the clinical situation, it may suggest that patients may not have, or be aware of, any inner emotional life themselves and therefore do not see it in others. They can therefore cause pain without guilt. More importantly, they may catch glimpses of integration and emotional aliveness in others, and this can arouse very powerful feelings of envy, which will inevitably be associated with destructive impulses (Joseph, 1986). Exploring the unconscious phantasies the patient may have in relation to the therapist may be helpful in indicating the presence of underlying envy. The way a patient reacts to a trial interpretation will give an indication of their ability to integrate their inner experience. Obviously such an interpretation must be carefully judged to be at a depth that is tolerable for the patient. Too deep an interpretation may produce a puzzled response or may alienate the patient completely; too superficial an interpretation will not test the strength of the personality. In other words, does the patient have the capacity to move from a paranoid–schizoid position to a depressive position through interpretation and understanding? If he is unable to do so, the interpretation will be perceived as threatening to the psyche and will result in a negative therapeutic reaction. Patients who survive by maintaining a borderline position or pathological organization (Steiner, 1987) are unable to tolerate any challenge to their delicate psychic equilibrium and may respond to interpretation and intimacy with psychic fragmentation and projection, the results of which are unpredictable.

Thus the details of the minute-to-minute dynamic changes and interventions will give an indication of how patients tolerate intimacy and psychic challenge and how they may defend themselves against linking and understanding. Assessment through the use of the trial interpretation must be done sensitively, as this produces anxiety, to which a small number of patients will react with anger.

Thus, in the clinical situation, an exploration of the personality structure, psychodynamics, defensive responses, and unconscious phantasy gives a picture of the potential for violence and the interpersonal triggers to such acts. Safety dictates that such an assessment must be done with at least some previous knowledge of the patient's history. The clinician's unconscious attitude is also important. He will bring a set of anxieties as well as his own personality structure, defences, and prejudices. An inappropriate countertransference reaction to a particular patient's projection or attitude can cause anything from negative therapeutic reaction to the arousal of rage. This does not mean that all clinicians should have an analysis, but it does make supervision and time for reflection essential.

Pathways of risk

The common view of risk is that it represents the likelihood of an event occurring in a given set of circumstances and that, given those circumstances, there is some predictability of that event reoccurring. However, this unidimensional approach ignores the complexity of the internal world and its interaction with the external environment. Levels of risk can fluctuate over very short periods of time, and therefore there is a need to conceptualize the processes that contribute to risk in systematic terms. It also assumes that risk is independent of the assessor. There are a great many knowable and unknowable factors that influence risk, and numerous decisions and interventions that occur in the assessment process can have an impact on the level of risk at any particular time. Some of those factors will be in the patient, some in the social circumstances of the patient, and some in the clinician.

Suicide and homicide are usually highly ambivalent acts, and the patient who experiences such impulses is likely to be ambivalent about the decision to seek help. For example, assuming the patient decides to seek help on a voluntary basis, the first port of call is likely to be his or her general practitioner. The patient has a paranoid psychosis, is very frightened, and does not know whom to trust. With the risk of disengagement at the back of his mind, the GP (general practitioner) has to decide how deeply to question the patient and whether to suggest referral on to specialist services. If she does not probe at all, it is very difficult to make a contract of treatment with the patient as he will be unable to agree a rational basis for the referral. If she does take a fuller history, it is done in the knowledge that at any point something she says may be misinterpreted, and she may alienate the patient. Having decided that specialist input is required, this has to be conveyed to the patient. If she believes that the patient will reject this suggestion, she may want to offer medication herself. At any point during this process of engagement, any rapport built up could break down. If the patient does disengage, then the GP must decide, with only fragments of evidence, whether to arrange a mental health act assessment—which has its own inherent risks.

Assuming the patient turns up at a specialist out-patient clinic, a similar process occurs with the psychiatrist or psychotherapist, and the same dilemmas are experienced. If the patient resists talking about certain areas of his life, do you push him further? Should diagnostic possibilities be discussed with the patient at the first interview? Until a rapport develops there is always the risk of disengagement. Once the patient has reluctantly accepted the need for medication, if that is appropriate, mention of side-effects may threaten the delicate trust that has developed, and yet failing to discuss the possibility may cause problems at a later date. The sensitivity of the clinician and her ability to listen to conscious and unconscious messages during this process is crucial. The initial assessment is clearly the most important contact the patient has with the system, and it must be managed carefully. It is the point at which patients can begin to develop trust in services and in individual clinicians, and to feel confident enough to form a treatment contract. On the other hand, if the patient finds difficulty in accessing services, is being passed between clinicians, or experiences a poorly managed initial consultation, any potential confidence is likely to be damaged. The patient is then lost, and if there is sufficient concern, he may need to be assertively followed up. This in itself will increase possible risks.

If we want people to come to us and tell us their deepest and most frightening anxieties, we must make their meeting with us safe and accessible. We must also ensure that clinicians feel safe and contained in order that they can encourage disclosure and explore the psychodynamics in the consultation.

Providing a safe environment for patient and clinician happens at several levels: the physical environment, the clinical contact, and the organizational attitude. The physical environment is important in terms of being welcoming and engaging. A dingy room at the back of an Accident and Emergency department, with furniture piled up, is unlikely to make the patient feel that his problem is important and that his presence is not merely an interference with much more important work. The consulting-room should be comfortable, non-arousing, and free from interruption. These simple rules apply, of course, to all consultations, but they are particularly important for the patient who is likely to be highly ambivalent about coming for help.

A good clinical contact depends on the level of competence of the practitioner, her training background, and her access to supervision. Clinicians also need to feel that if something does go wrong, such an incident will be investigated in an open and supportive manner and that the process is not one in which scapegoats will be sought.

Organizations, and particularly multi-professional teams, are always open to and at risk of splitting, particularly by destructive patients. An unhealthy team where communication is rigid and sparse, where there are schisms between professions, and where management is weak can increase risks. Poor communication about levels of risk can leave practitioners vulnerable and ultimately can lead to untoward incidents.

Again a common theme of many homicide and suicide enquiries focuses on poor communication between professions and social and health agencies. More importantly, such a team is fertile ground on which to act out the projections of disturbed patients, particularly those patients with strong borderline elements to their personalities. Teams that do not have systems in place for good communication of information are likely to reflect the psychic fragmentation of their patients, leading to a deterioration of any communication processes that do exist. The outcome of such a situation is that the patients' worst fears about the inability of parental figures to contain their destructive impulses is realized and they can become frightened and hopeless and may be potentially violent. Patients will always project their psychopathology into teams. What is important is the team's ability to reflect on and contain such psychopathology through good communication and the ability to agree on a set of interventions that are corporately held. Individual clinicians will then have the ability to implement an intervention with confidence, and the patient will experience containment.

A particularly important facet of clinical safety for practitioners is knowing that if the anxiety of a consultation or of the relationship with the patient becomes uncontainable, there will be a process whereby the situation can be made safe. A common barrier in health services is that between general psychiatry, who have control over in-patient beds, and psychotherapists and psychology services, who often have no access to in-patient beds. If we expect psychological therapists to assess and to treat potentially suicidal or dangerous patients, it is essential that there is a mechanism whereby the services of general psychiatry can be accessed quickly and easily.

Conclusions

Mental health practitioners are given and accept an ambiguous task. They are expected to care for and to help the patient with mental illness at the same time as taking responsibility for coming to a judgement about the patient's likelihood of committing violence to themselves or others. Assessing and containing that risk is most effectively done by an organization that understands its responsibilities and creates a supportive system around its front-line clinicians, and a clinician who has the appropriate level of training and experience and a process that is thoughtful and structured. Such measures not only make risk assessment an understandable and manageable part of clinical work but also have the effect of reducing risk *per se*. However, what has been described here could be said to constitute any good mental health service, and a study of recent inquiries concluded that, of those homicides considered preventable, this would have been achieved by improving mental health services in general rather than improving risk assessment alone (Munro & Rumgay, 2000).

CHAPTER TWO

Assessment of violence
in medium-secure units

Ian Treasaden

Medium-secure units are for those with mental disorder whose disruptive and/or dangerous behaviour requires psychiatric treatment in conditions of greater security than is provided in ordinary hospitals, including locked local secure and intensive care units, but less than in special hospitals. Most units take predominantly male individuals suffering from severe psychotic mental illness, particularly paranoid schizophrenia, who have dangerously offended—for example, those charged with manslaughter, wounding with intent to cause grievous bodily harm, and arson with intent. It was intended that aggressive psychopaths and the severely mentally impaired should be excluded, but, though medium-secure units rarely take those with a legal diagnosis of psychopathic disorder directly, they each do take a number of such individuals as a graded step in their rehabilitation from special hospitals.

Although medium-secure units are generally funded for their in-patient services, much of their work involves the assessment elsewhere of mentally abnormal offenders, often for courts, or of other individuals who are not formally charged with offences but whose behaviour gives rise to concern that they might pose serious risk to others.

Patients in a medium-secure unit receive modified milieu therapy within a containing and physically secure and structured setting, and patients are involved as much as possible in the running of the unit. This environment can offer emotional and physical security for individuals who had previously led insecure and chaotic lives. In particular, it can help to provide containment of intolerable feelings of pain, hatred, and envy that a patient might be at risk of projecting. Powerful hostile transference feelings tend to be more intense and violent in those with severe psychotic mental illness, among whom there is a corresponding greater danger of acting out.

Medium-secure units

Individuals in medium-secure units are usually detained primarily for the protection of others, but they may be also detained for the sake of their own health and/or safety. Most will have been convicted of their index offence or offences but sentenced to detention in hospital, usually with a restriction order without time limit, which allows discharge with conditions, as an alternative to a custodial sentence. They are thus removed from the penal to the medical system, where release depends not on the expiry of a fixed, determinate sentence, but on improvement of their mental disorder. This means that they have to convince their psychiatric supervisors that they are mentally well, have good insight into their index offences, their mental disorder, and their need for treatment, and are no longer a risk to others. Such individuals may regret not having a fixed sentence at the end of which they could be certain that they would be discharged. Some are transferred from prison to medium-secure units, either while on remand awaiting trial and/or sentence or during a subsequent prison sentence as a result of having developed a mental illness. The latter may be due to the stress of imprisonment, or it may be that their mental disorder was missed at the time of their trial. A few may be so unwell that they are detained after being found in court to be unfit to plead or not guilty by reason of insanity.

Those charged with murder, which carries a mandatory life sentence, may have their charge reduced to one of manslaughter on grounds of diminished responsibility and subsequently be sentenced to be detained under a hospital order, usually with a restriction order without time limit, in a medium-secure unit or a special hospital. Most individuals who have killed do not regard themselves as typical murderers, and many resent the implications of the word "manslaughter". Nevertheless, while murderous thoughts can be normal, acting on them is not. Homicide can often be seen as preventing something psychologically worse happening to the offending individual. Such offenders may initially idolize their victims after the offence, which may delay the therapist being able to accurately assess their motivation for their offence and future risk.

Feigning madness to avoid legal consequences is, in fact, very rare. Most who are suspected of doing so are subsequently found to be genuinely mentally disordered. It is very difficult for individuals to feign symptoms on a sustained basis and in a way that is characteristic of particular mental illnesses. Such individuals, instead, usually behave in a manner based on their own lay ideas of how the mentally ill present. Fear of madness and of being administered psychotropic medication—not least because it may adversely affect their sexual functioning—deters many from seeking psychiatric help or a psychiatric disposal in court.

Amnesia does not in itself constitute a defence in court. Apart from organic causes such as head injury or epilepsy, it may reflect lying or voluntary intoxication with alcohol and/or drugs, which generally is also not a defence in itself. However, 40–50% of those convicted of homicide claim amnesia of the offence. This may reflect hysterical denial or hysterical amnesia, even in the face of having been found with "blood on their hands". Subsequently, however, many such individuals acknowledge that they had always been able to recall committing the offence, but they state that it was initially too painful to think or talk about. Others may recall the circumstances before and after the index offence but never the actual incident itself, due to over-arousal, such as intense anger at the time of the offence, preventing memory registration.

Terminology: *Violence* is action, while *dangerousness* is a potential and a matter of opinion. The term *risk* is now being used increasingly in professional practice in preference to dangerousness. Risk is, ideally, a matter of statistical fact. It suggests a continuum of levels of risk, varying not only with the individual but also with the context. It may change rapidly over time and, in principle, should be based on objective assessment. Dangerousness tends to imply an all-or-none phenomenon and a static characteristic of an individual. However, clearly *risk assessment* is less important than *risk management*, though risk management does not imply *risk elimination*.

Violence and mental illness

Violence is multifactorially caused and is a bio-psycho-social-environmental phenomenon. Clearly all behaviour has a biochemical basis, but while biochemical abnormalities can cause psychological symptoms, including aggression, there is also increasing evidence that psychological events, such as severe abuse in childhood and severe psychological trauma in adulthood, may cause neuro-biological abnormalities, such as serotonin metabolism—in adults. It is important to be aware that no model of aggression fits all individuals.

Lorenz (1966) noted that a personal bond and individual friendship is found only in animals with highly developed intraspecific aggression. In fact, the firmer the bond, the more aggressive the particular animal or species is. Real intimacy thus may occur only when individuals share real aggressive and good feelings.

If there is a direct relationship between a patient's violence and his mental illness, control of the mental illness should reduce, if not remove, the risk of violence in future. However, if there are compounding problems, such as personality disorder, drug abuse, post-traumatic stress symptoms or disorder, brain damage, or epilepsy, control of positive psychotic symptoms of mental illness alone may not be sufficient to remove the risk of violence. In individuals with a personality disorder it may be particularly difficult to assess both the risk to others and their motivation and amenability to treatment, and such patients have been some of the most notorious failures of special hospitals.

In the past, factors associated with violence—for example, personality disorder, impulsivity, anger, violent family background, and substance abuse—were said to be the same whether or not the offender was mentally ill. However, evidence over the past decade has shown that having a diagnosis of mental illness is weakly associated with violence due to a sub-group having specific types of symptoms, such as paranoid delusions and delusions of passivity (being under external control). These findings are in keeping with social psychology theories that violence in general is associated with an individual feeling under threat or losing control of his situation.

Individuals with affective disorders are under-represented in medium-secure units, whereas patients with schizophrenia are over-represented, especially among those who drift out of treatment. Violence can arise directly from positive symptoms of mental illness. Mental illness may, however, indirectly lead to violence through associated deterioration in social functioning and personality. Such individuals become more antisocial and impulsive, with a lower tolerance of stress, and they may wrongly be given an additional diagnosis of personality disorder to explain their violence. A mentally ill individual may also behave violently for "normal" emotional reasons, such as fear and anger, but may then experience accompanying corresponding psychotic symptoms, such as auditory hallucinations with aggressive content. Violence, involvement with the law, and imprisonment may themselves precipitate mental illness.

Psychodynamic issues in risk assessment

Risk assessment can only be a probability assessment. Dangerous behaviour is rare and sporadic, and most of our worries about individuals never materialize. This can lull professionals into a false sense of security and cause them to underestimate the risk. However, false positive assessments of risk are more common than are false negative ones. Assessors tend to err on the side of caution and may also be reluctant to take on individuals considered at serious risk of harming others. The assessor may feel shocked and overwhelmed by the patient's past offences or be afraid of being held professionally responsible for the individual's actions. Such negative countertransference can lead to the overestimation of risks and to inappropriate and precipitate actions to cover the assessor and to displace responsibility onto others. On other occasions, professionals may feel impelled to "rescue" dangerous, untreatable individuals who, they feel, have been badly managed by others. A designated specialist psychotherapist may be asked to advise on the assessment and management. Even if specific psychotherapeutic treatment is not indicated, the psychotherapist may provide valuable psychodynamic understanding of the individual and of his risk to others and insight into the countertransference.

Psychodynamic insight may be of value in deciding when certain individuals should be transferred or discharged. However, given the therapeutic nature of their relationship with the individual, psychotherapists should not be involved directly in providing reports to courts, mental health review tribunals, or the Home Office. Some therapists prefer to keep details of their therapeutic work confidential, even from the multidisciplinary team, providing information about general progress and other issues on a need-to-know basis only. Others adopt a more integrated approach, informing the multidisciplinary team of all aspects of assessment and progress, which may mean that the patient is less open in working through his difficulties, fearing that what he tells his therapist may be held against him in terms of his progress.

All patients have what they consider to be valid reasons for their aggressive behaviour. However, they often want a reaction to it, including, on occasion, containment. The aim is to understand and respond appropriately to the violence. Otherwise the patient may feel incompetent and merely escalate his dangerous behaviour. Violent patients often have more control than is apparent. In many situations they could have behaved more dangerously; at some level there are boundaries they won't cross in relating to their carers. Aggression is often multidetermined; some motives are conscious, others are concealed and unconscious.

Following a violent incident in hospital, it is useful to consider what the staff may have done, albeit unwittingly, to provoke such behaviour. Exploring this element with the patient can lead to an increased understanding of the individual's propensity for violence in the context of his past traumas and resulting over-sensitivities. Sometimes staff may be reluctant to address their own contribution, preferring to concentrate on managing the patient rather than understanding his actions. Indeed, institutions risk becoming primarily designed to contain the anxiety of staff (Menzies Lyth, 1988). However, staff may also react by inappropriately blaming themselves if they have been assaulted by patients. This may reflect a human evolutionary defence mechanism against being at the mercy of an unpredictable world.

For accurate risk assessment, it is immensely helpful for all members of the multidisciplinary team to be aware of the primitive defence mechanisms of splitting and projective identification (Klein, 1946). Patients may project their bad parts into authority, leading to a "them-or-us" attitude to the assessor. This may also be reflected in the way they may perceive themselves to have been unfairly treated by the courts and in hospital. Splitting also occurs between staff: for example, nursing staff may be hated while the consultant psychiatrist or the psychotherapist may be regarded as good and the only one who understands.

Mentally abnormal offenders are often unable to accept full responsibility for their index offences and will try to blame others or, alternatively, may inappropriately attribute the entire causation of their offending, when this is not the case, to a mental illness from which they have now recovered. Classically, offenders have been considered to have weak superegos, and mental illness itself can result in a functionally weak superego. However, other offenders have harsh, punitive superegos, which means that they can be hard on themselves and on the professionals. Patients, especially those with personality disorders, are in any case likely to be ambivalent and, on occasion, hostile about their need for psychological help and in their attitude to it. Staff need to maintain their judgement in spite of their own anxiety about the patient or his index offence, and they must avoid both over-identification with the offender and denial of his dangerousness. Conflicts can arise, particularly for nursing staff, between their individual risk assessment and therapeutic work with a patient, which may involve encouraging the expression of strong emotions, and their role with others in keeping the unit safe, which may require the suppression of the patient's strong and hostile feelings by medication and seclusion.

The process of risk assessment and risk management may be facilitated by counselling, supportive psychotherapy, or more in-depth individual and group psychotherapeutic work. Issues of risk are often highlighted not only by what the patient says but what he does not say, and the work allows an exploration of the degree to which the patient minimizes, denies, or suppresses the enormity of what he has done and the risk of his behaving in such a way in the future. It can also allow the individual to work through and undo past experiences, to adjust to the reality of his offence with its associated guilt, and to lessen projective identification. On a practical level, this may involve the patient learning to take responsibility for managing his own illness through accepting his need for treatment and increasing his awareness of risk factors.

Those who have been abused often identify with the aggressor. Such individuals have a need to make the object of their attachment good, even when that object has abused them. Their own feelings of badness and guilt may result in a need for punishment and be dramatized in violence at the time of their index offence or offences, or in a pattern of self-defeating behaviours reflecting repetition compulsion. Aggression may be displaced into formal complaints and litigiousness, including allegations of physical harm by staff. The assessor may be subject to projective identification resulting in an inappropriate response, which may be reflected in written records and reports, and reinforce the perception of the assessor by the patient as another abuser.

Non-verbal therapies, such as art, drama, and music therapy, may also assist in risk assessment and management, particularly for those who find it difficult to express their feelings in verbal form. Drama therapy may provide insight into the patient's empathy with the victim through using, for instance, the empty-chair technique or through sculpting the dynamics of his family.

A psychodynamic model of risk assessment

Risk assessment aims to get an understanding of the risk from a detailed historical longitudinal overview obtained not only from the patient, who may minimize his past history, but from independent informants and records. It has been argued that risk assessment should always involve a psychodynamic formulation, given that actuarial models of risk assessment based on epidemiology and statistics alone are insufficient. In the Jason Mitchell inquiry (Bloom-Cooper, Grounds, Guinan, Parker, & Taylor, 1996, p. 170), it was argued that in-patient units with patients who include offenders with disturbed personalities should have access to specialist psychodynamic expertise. A psychodynamic formulation may, for example, include a history of childhood trauma, a lack of ability to tolerate and contain resulting painful feelings, precipitating circumstances perceived as a repetition of earlier trauma, and projection and violent acting out of an individual's internal world and objects.

Violence may be a form of communication, or a symptom of high emotional arousal, or it may have a psychodynamic meaning. Did the patient rationalize his behaviour—for instance, in terms of whether it was planned, impulsive or provoked? Was the violence committed alone or in groups where there is less inhibition? Were there triggers—such as behavioural, emotional, physiological, or situational ones, for example? Was the violence part of other criminal behaviour? Was it an act of deliberate self-harm? What caused it to cease? Did the offender summon help? Did the violence represent displaced aggression (e.g. a mother kills a baby to spite the father)?

What were the individual's mental state and feelings at the time of the violence? Was the violence linked to specific symptoms—to paranoid delusions or delusions of passivity (threat/control override symptoms), for example, or to over-arousal, anxiety, fear, irritability, anger, suspiciousness, or disinhibition? Had there been a recent discontinuation of medication?

In general, the more fragile the psychological defences, the greater the violence. The degree of violence is often not predictive of repetition but reflects the relationship with the victim: for example, the resistance of the victim to dying or the arousal of the offender. It is also important to elucidate if satisfaction was derived from inflicting pain. Current stressors, particularly life events of recent loss or threat of loss, may have been crucial to precipitating the violence. Disruption of the therapeutic alliance—through professional holidays, for example—may be one such stressor. It is important to elucidate if such precipitating factors have now been removed or can be modified.

Regarding the victim, it is important to establish whether the violence is directed against a particular individual for a specific reason, against a particular type of victim (e.g., staff), a particular institution, or the world in general, or is that person merely the object of aggression displaced from others, such as mother or society? Is the victim the real intended victim? With such displacement, there is clearly a risk of repetition.

The way the individual talks about his violence and his victim is important. Is he dispassionate or guilty? Does he have a capacity for sympathetic identification? One should be aware of protective psychological defence mechanisms, which may lead to apparent callous indifference. Overall, admission of guilt and transparency are considered favourable factors; unfavourable signs include regression after an offence, amnesia, and an attitude of "unfinished business".

For more accurate risk assessment, interviews or psychotherapeutic assessment sessions should take place on more than one occasion and be repeated periodically. At interview, expressed threats of violence are more important than generalized verbal anger. A feeling of fear in the interviewer may be important, but it needs to be interpreted in the light of transference and countertransference phenomena. The content of delusions or hallucinations may be meaningful in terms of underlying conflicts. There may be a contrast between a patient's apparent passivity and an inner experience, such as auditory hallucinations (voices) telling him to kill, which reflects the psychological fragmentation seen in psychosis. In those with schizophrenia, concrete thinking may have been a factor in past violence, and it can lead to such individuals interpreting staff comments literally. The level of insight of the individual into his mental disorder and offending needs to be ascertained. Does he regard violence as unacceptable? Is he attempting self-control? Does he request help? In the assessment interview, emphasis on the here-and-now may be more useful for gauging the level of insight than exploration of family and early background.

Conclusions

An assessment based on psychodynamic principles should therefore allow the assessor to build up a picture of the degree of risk, its nature and magnitude, whether it is specific or general, conditional or unconditional, immediate, long-term, or volatile, and who might be in danger from the patient in the future. Following a risk assessment, a risk-management plan, ideally agreed with the individual, should be developed to modify the risk factors and specify response triggers. Enquiries into homicides have highlighted not the limitations of risk assessment, real as these are, but failure to communicate or to manage known risks.

CHAPTER THREE

Risk assessment
in general psychiatry:
a psychoanalytic perspective

Richard Lucas

We are living through changing times in general psychiatry, with the closure of the large mental hospitals and a shift in emphasis to community care. This move has resulted in a fall in the availability of acute beds and a feeling of insecurity about containing more disturbed patients in the community. Tragedies have occurred, and these have heightened anxieties and led to an increase in bureaucracy, in the hope of replacing the asylum walls with walls of paper. The strain on professional staff can lead to burn out, premature retirement, and a fear of reprisals if administrative dictates have not been followed to the letter.

At the same time it is known that, however laudable the aims, risk-assessment forms and Care Programme Approach (CPA) meetings alone do not prevent tragedies. Risk assessment remains based at a clinical level, each case having to be considered on its own merits. In such a situation, it is important to have clinically relevant frameworks of understanding when facing disturbing and potentially unpredictable acting-out behaviour. The frameworks should also provide containment for the staff's anxieties and help in living with difficult situations and in recognizing our human limitations.

Acquiring relevant frameworks of understanding involves an ongoing individual learning curve for all those working in the field of general psychiatry. In this chapter, the writer shares some of the frameworks that he has found helpful when presented with challenging situations and shows how psychoanalytic insights form the core of these ways of thinking.

Three areas of particular concern are considered: namely, violence directed at others, violence directed at the self (suicidal acts), and the effect of such incidents on staff morale. In contrast to other recent analytic contributions on violence (Perelberg, 1999), attention here is focused on the more extreme psychotic states of mind encountered in everyday general psychiatry.

The first clinical examples illustrate the potential to underrate the dangerousness of psychotic states and the need to employ a sound underlying theoretical framework. A case of inpatient suicide is then described, including the management's response and the effect on the staff.

In the discussion, I consider ways of reducing risks of escalation of violence and of coping with tragedies. More open dialogue between fellow professionals, developing a well-functioning, analytically informed, integrated approach at the ward level, and supporting staff when inevitable tragedies occur are seen as ways forward.

Assessment of potential violence in psychotic states

Many interesting statistics have arisen from the National Confidential Inquiry into homicides and suicides in people with mental illness (Appleby, 1997; Thompson, 1999). Of those who had committed homicides, the majority had personality disorders, often abetted by drug or alcohol abuse; fewer had schizophrenia. Overall, most victims were within the perpetrators' families or were otherwise known to them. However, with psychotic patients who present a considerable challenge in determining the risk of potential violence, the violent act might be towards a complete stranger.

If persecutory or depressive feelings become unbearable, the psychotic patient may project the problem concretely into a stranger and then seek relief through attacking him. Sohn described the process in detail with an analytic study of patients who attempted to push strangers onto railway lines (Sohn, 1997).

While risk assessment takes place every time a patient with a history of psychosis is seen clinically, in two particular settings this is the central feature of the proceedings: when assessing the grounds for a formal hospital admission, and when a hospital tribunal is considering whether it is safe to lift a restriction order.

For a patient to be admitted on a compulsory basis under the mental health act, it requires a recommendation from two doctors. Ideally, one should be the patient's general practitioner (GP), who knows the patient well, and the other should be a specialist in psychiatry, ideally the responsible consultant. The approved social worker (ASW), after speaking with the nearest relative and seeing the patient, then decides whether to complete the section. In most cases, there is full agreement on the necessity for a formal admission. However, in cases where problems have arisen, lessons can be learned. The following case serves as an illustration.

"Mr A"

Mr A, a patient with a previous record of admission in a violent psychotic state, was noted by his mother to be deteriorating. He had stopped complying with his medication, he would no longer allow her access to his residence, and she noted, through his window, broken dishes in his bedroom. His mother notified the Community Mental Health Nurse (CMHN), but the patient threatened to harm the CMHN if she attempted to visit.

The CMHN notified the GP, and, as the responsible psychiatric consultant, I was requested to go on a domiciliary visit. The patient was clearly in a guarded and paranoid state, only allowing a limited dialogue in the hallway. I completed my part of a compulsory order. The GP did not visit, as the patient's current residence was some distance from his practice. The ASW came with another doctor, approved under the act but previously unfamiliar with the patient. The patient was still guarded in manner, refusing access to his room on the grounds that one's privacy should be respected. He described his mother as having a poor understanding of his needs, but he agreed that he should not have spoken in the described manner to the CMHN. The patient said to the ASW that he would be visiting his GP that week to collect further medication and would comply with out-patient attendance. In such a situation, it was felt that the order could not be completed. It was also suggested by the ASW that the mother might need help to improve her understanding of her son. The following day, after an unprovoked act of violence towards a stranger in the community, the patient was appre-hended and then hospitalized.

This brief vignette raises several issues for consideration, aside from the immediate points that the GP, who knew the patient, was not able to be part of the assessment team and that the ASW had not spoken directly with the consultant before arriving at his decision.

Patients with psychotic disorders project and disown their problematic states of mind, especially when relapsing. The com-monest presenting symptom of psychosis is not hallucinations or delusions, which are found in some 60% of cases, but lack of insight presenting as denial and rationalization, which is found in over 90% of cases (Gelder et al., 1998).

It is helpful to think of two separately functioning parts to the mind—namely, the psychotic and non-psychotic parts, as de-scribed by Bion (1957). While the non-psychotic part is capable of reflection, the psychotic part, fuelled by envy and hatred of psychic reality, operates by evacuating troublesome feelings, thereby creat-ing hallucinations and delusions. The psychotic part then covers up its murderous activity by appearing calm and reasonable. Each time we have to make an assessment of a patient with a suggested history of psychosis, Bion invites us to consider whether we are hearing a straightforward communication from the non-psychotic part or being invited to accept a rationalization from the psychotic part.

Bion's theory provides an analytic framework which helps in our understanding of this vignette. In physical illnesses it is the doctor who makes the diagnosis. With a relapse of psychosis, it is the relative who makes the initial diagnosis. It is then a case of whether the professionals will believe them or accept the patient's denial of illness and rationalized explanations for his reported disturbed behaviour. Without Bion's model in mind, one may be forced into a position, as occurred in this case, of adopting a moral stance in which the relative is held to be in the wrong. This can result in underestimating the degree of potential violence.

The development of a psychoanalytic understanding of psychosis has mirrored the issues raised by this case. Classically, many analysts have maintained an undifferentiated approach to neurosis and psychosis. Frieda Fromm-Reichmann, an eminent American analyst, wrote: "It is my belief that the problems and emotional difficulties of mental patients, neurotics or psychotics, are in principle rather similar to one another and also the emotional difficulties from which we all suffer"(Fromm-Reichmann, 1950). Adopting this attitude may invite one to take the patient's communications at face value, as describing a true state of affairs.

Another group of analysts developed a different theoretical understanding, taking the view of a continuum from neurosis to psychosis, including a pre-psychotic and psychotic phase (Yorke, 1991). In the pre-psychotic phase, emotional conflict produces regressive behaviour of a neurotic kind, whereas in the psychotic phase there is a temporary fragmentation of the ego. This theory explains how temporary fragmented states of mind can occur under stress—the so-called psychogenic or reactive psychoses. What the theory does not do is to differentiate the major psychotic disorders, such as schizophrenia, from short-lived reactive states.

Again referring to the clinical vignette, it is important to decide whether one is dealing with a transient disturbed outburst, as the ASW felt, or with the early stages of a more persistent psychotic relapse. In drawing attention to the particular and persisting psychopathology underlying schizophrenia, Bion invites us to consider this as an alternative explanation for the patient's behaviour.

Another place where the severity of the psychopathology can be underrated is the mental health review tribunal. Usually these are straightforward, but occasionally cases arise that require further debate. The following serves as such an example.

"Mrs B"

I was asked to make a home visit to a patient, Mrs B, who had a recent history of unprovoked attacks on visiting care workers, who had been concerned about her ability to look after her children. I saw her in the company of her husband, who explained my presence to the patient. At first she sat mute and unresponsive. She then suddenly stood up, went into the kitchen, and returned wielding a large plank of wood, with which she attacked me. I managed to escape relatively unscathed. It was the weekend, and I was left feeling somewhat guilty about how disturbed she might become once admitted, fearing that the nursing staff would then be on the receiving end of her violence.

However, following admission to hospital on a formal basis, she presented no management problem at all on the ward. When I saw her on the Monday, she presented in a calm state in which she rationalized her previously aggressive behaviour. She said that she had intended to break my skull, and that anyone would have acted in a similar fashion towards a stranger coming into their house without wearing a name tab! She also expressed a grandiose delusion of owning her street. Her husband furnished a history of her being ill for several years.

A chance finding on testing was a low thyroxine level. She appealed against her section. At the tribunal, attended by my junior doctor, the tribunal doctor attributed her mental state entirely to an under-functioning thyroid and said that she could take the treatment of replacement hormone at home—even though the doctor had been fully informed on the background history. The lay people on the tribunal accepted the medical opinion and discharged the patient from her section, engendering our considerable concern. When I voiced my disagreement with the judgement to the local regional chairman of tribunals, it transpired that there was no mechanism for feedback of my concern to the tribunal, since it had disbanded after coming to its conclusion. Furthermore, the government did not provide funding for update learning for tribunal members in such cases.

"Myxoedemic madness" arising from a low-functioning thyroid is a very rare condition indeed, and a much less likely diagnosis than that of a paranoid schizophrenic illness. Here the issue is not of an

ASW being persuaded by the patient to see things his way, but of the lay members of a tribunal accepting uncritically the doctor's view. The patient's current potential dangerousness, regardless of possible medical diagnosis, was ignored. We all carry a desire within ourselves for an all-embracing answer so we may avoid facing indescribably difficult psychotic states of mind, and we need to monitor ourselves at all times to ensure that we are not falling for some seductively welcome rationalization. This is the lesson from the two cases.

Violence to self: an inpatient suicide

We also need frameworks for understanding suicidal states of mind, and for helping to keep anxieties within manageable proportions.

"Mrs C"

Mrs C was a middle-aged woman with a ten-year history of unremitting severe psychotic depression. Many years ago she had jumped onto a railway line and had lost both legs. Since then there had been further suicide attempts, one through swallowing weed-killer and several others through taking overdoses.

Following the overdoses, there would be periods in hospital, with her being admitted on a section. She would never discuss the suicide attempts. She would just fix the doctor with a chillingly murderous stare. She would also have screaming fits on the ward. These were not amenable to discussion but would subside prior to her discharge back into the community.

We spoke at length with her husband about the outlook, saying that one day she was likely to kill herself, and we all agreed we could only do our best. While in hospital, the nursing staff and occupational therapist found it hard to engage her in any activity; the only sign of life was an interest in playing games of Scrabble. My countertransference feelings when on the receiving end of the chilling stare led me to understand the underlying dynamics in terms of a dominating murderous psychotic part keeping imprisoned another part of her which wanted human contact—that is, through the Scrabble games.

When Mrs C returned home, she tended to lie passively downstairs with her elderly mother in attendance, until the next admission. When I put it to her that there was an imprisoned part that wanted us to help bring some variety into her life when she was out of hospital, a tear trickled down her cheek. She said that she would like to be taken swimming. We said we would make arrangements for a befriender to take her, when she was settled enough to return home. The CPA programme was fully in place and recorded.

Two weeks before her death, she stayed behind while other patients went on a day trip to the seaside. The bus couldn't accommodate her wheelchair. She appeared angry. While she was bathing her, the nurse went to get a towel. In that moment, she submerged under the water, giving the nurse a fright as she pulled her up. This bathroom also contained a toilet, the only one on the ward wide enough to accommodate her wheelchair and so allow her to get independently onto the toilet. Over the next 24 hours her mood settled. She continued, as previously, to go independently to that toilet. Within two weeks, it was felt by all that she was ready for a trial weekend at home. Her husband came on the Saturday morning to collect her. She had gone to the toilet. While in there, she had turned on the bath and drowned herself.

It was the reaction to the event that is of particular interest. I had been away on leave and returned to face an internal hospital inquiry. Understandably, the management was required to investigate and look for any lessons to be learned. For example, was the CPA form completed and had it been reviewed recently? Did everyone know its content? Did another nurse become the key worker if the key worker was not on duty? Was there adequate interdisciplinary communication? Could the ward be altered in design to enhance safety?

However, with the degree of anxiety engendered and pressures to produce a report with recommendations, there is a danger that practical questions such as these become regarded as possible explanations to account for the tragedy. The nursing staff, who had cared for the patient and were devastated by her death, inevitably then experienced themselves as being on the receiving end of a clinical inquiry. I saw it as the consultant's role to support the nursing staff and to attempt to bring in a balanced perspective: namely, that while an inquiry must be made and any lessons learned, there was still the possibility that the tragedy was nobody's fault and could not have been prevented. It was interesting to consider my superego or critical conscience, which I felt answerable to in that situation, as the consultant. In my mind, the arbitrator would be an understanding coroner.

Fortunately, in this case the coroner proved to be non-judgemental. He apportioned no blame or criticism but expressed sympathy to all those affected by the tragedy. Coming up to me afterwards, he gave the opinion that the patient's condition had been untreatable. It was not the first time that I have experienced a coroner, as the representative of the law, being understanding rather than critical of staff in such circumstances.

Coming to terms with suicides

In his classical paper "Mourning and Melancholia" (1917e [1915]), Freud described how, after a loss, we all have to go through the work of mourning. We have to accept the person's death and, by going over personal experiences, reinstate our memory of them inside us. Later losses, as Klein pointed out, bring to our minds losses earlier in life, especially if there are unresolved issues (Klein, 1940).

The finality of the suicidal act, however, makes us more likely to react like Freud's description of the melancholic. Rather than being able to mourn the unbearable pain of the situation, it leads us to attribute blame to ourselves or to others. As described by Bion (1962b), this might be viewed as the presence of a primitive, severe, ego-destructive superego that temporarily usurps the position normally occupied in our mind by a more benign, mature, reflective superego that tolerates the complexities of life—the coroner in my story.

In her classical work, *The Ego and the Mechanisms of Defence* (1936), Anna Freud described how we all have ways of unconsciously warding off unbearable anxieties and guilt through such processes as projection, displacement, intellectualization, and rationalization. Being aware that such forces operate within ourselves may help us to contain our anxieties rather than to project blame onto others in such extreme situations.

Suicide challenges our omnipotent beliefs that we can help everybody and that we could have prevented the tragedy, if only we had carried out the right practice. It is particularly hard on nursing staff, who have given loving care to a patient over many admissions, to try to come to terms with a suicide, while also having to answer to the immediate internal inquiry. Awareness of the accumulated general psychiatric knowledge on suicides, in conjunction with some related analytic insights, may help with our thinking when faced with these tragic events.

Stengel (1946) found that statistically suicides fell into two main groupings: the attempted (para-suicide) and the suicide proper. Patients in the former group were younger, and there were more females; the overdose was seen as a cry for help, combined with a wish for temporary oblivion as an escape from problems. Typically, the family then rallied round. Occasionally, however, unforeseen tragedies can occur. I recall a young man who took an overdose of only ten Paracetamol tablets after a row with his girlfriend. They made it up, but he died a few days later of an allergic hepatitis. Improved treatment techniques may nowadays reduce such outcomes.

Stengel's group of "suicide proper" were typically elderly, male, and socially isolated, with physical disabilities and symptoms of a major depressive illness or melancholia (in Freud's terminology.) We now know that 50% of them have visited their GPs in the weeks before the suicide.

Freud described the presence in all of us of both self-preservative life forces and self-destructive drives, the latter being linked with his concept of an innate death instinct (Freud, 1920g). Usually our emotional states contain a mixture of positive and negative feelings. However, at times of suicidal and other violent acts, there is a defusion of the two forces, with the destructive force in the ascendancy.

Paradoxically, when adolescents attack their own bodies in an attempted suicide, it can be viewed as a self-preservative act: the bad frustrating object has been temporarily projected into the body (Laufer & Laufer, 1984). This dynamic may occur also in more extreme conditions. A patient of mine described how, during a puerperal psychosis, she had to fight the urge to kill her baby daughter. She felt that she should kill her to prevent her from having no life, as the baby reminded her of her mother's stillbirth. Instead she cut her own wrists but fortunately then sought help. Here the suicidal thoughts are again paradoxically linked with a preservative aim (Lucas, 1994).

An opposite picture may be presented in some cases of suicidal states of mind arising in schizophrenia. Again in this context, I have found Bion's concept of psychotic and non-psychotic parts of the personality helpful (Bion, 1957). I came to realize how a patient had jumped out of a window, not in a state of despair, but because she felt pushed out by an intolerant psychotic part of herself. This accounted for the fact that she presented afterwards in a frightened state. The non-psychotic part of the patient was communicating to us her fear of being the victim of a murderously intolerant psychotic part (Lucas, 1992).

In some cases of suicide, one might view the death instinct as producing death to avoid having to account for its own destructiveness. One might look at the inpatient suicide I described in those terms—that is, the more open state, emerging with her tears, leading to her becoming vulnerable to a defensive deadly backlash.

Discussion

Considering ways forward

Recent articles continue to reinforce the view that there is no foolproof way to prevent tragedies. In a review entitled "Face to Face with the Suicidal", Morgan, Buckley, and Nowers (1998), write: "Failure to predict suicide should not be regarded as necessarily related to a poor standard of clinical care." In a study of "One hundred in-patient suicides" Proulx, Lesage, and Grunberg (1997), commented in summary: "Inpatient suicides remain a relatively rare phenomenon, difficult to predict, and that all the signs of a potentially impending suicide can be identified more easily with the benefit of hindsight" (p. 250).

However, the desire to achieve an anxiety-free state in relation to potential violent acts, whether directed at oneself or at others, has resulted in an irresistible momentum to introduce risk-assessment forms. Proulx and colleagues commented: "If used prospectively, suicide risk scales carry the risk of identifying a large number of false positives, and our study could not find any specific item which would improve the specificity of such scales." The concern remains that the institutional pressures to introduce such scales may create a defensive attitude in the staff to protect against potential criticism.

Amongst the recommendations for improvement was a suggested thorough overhaul of the CPA, and training in risk assessment. However, as has been already discussed, when it comes to individual cases, we will still have to rely on our own sensitivities and clinical acumen.

What, then, is the way forward? I think that we can find some guidance in the recommendations made in "The Falling Shadow— A Report on a Homicide Enquiry commissioned by the South Devon Health Care Trust" (1995). The report was on a patient who fatally wounded a hospital-based occupational therapist.

While exploring areas of concern, the members of the enquiry were at pains to point out that good practice relies on good morale. This means a feeling among practitioners that they will be supported if they act reasonably, given the circumstances known to exist at the time when a decision is taken, even when the decisions have unfortunate, even catastrophic, consequences. The enquiry team stressed that risk cannot be avoided, and that "the occurrence of such tragedies does not *per se* demonstrate any error of judgement". The investigating group accepted that the incident under consideration was "inherently unpredictable".

Of course, this does not refute the fact that with all incidents of violence there are aspects to be explored and lessons to be learned.

The introduction of CPA meetings and designated key workers were steps taken to ensure that there was designated follow-up care of patients with vulnerable states of mind. In the examples given earlier, one can see areas for improvement in ASW training and in the monitoring of the mental health review tribunals. The central issue is the need to maintain the right balance between support and inquiry.

Confidentiality and psychosis

Better understanding involves an open sharing of concerns about unpredictable behaviour with patients, their relatives, and fellow professional staff. This raises an important principle: the issue of confidentiality in psychosis. Normally, patient confidentiality would be preserved at all times between patient and carer, especially in the psychotherapy situation. However, even the British Psychoanalytical Society recognizes in its ethical code and guidelines that psychosis may prove an exception in carefully considered cases, and inappropriate withholding of information may sometimes lead to an otherwise avoidable traumatic incident.

Patients in psychotic states tend to fragment and project their feelings, and different people pick up different bits, like pieces of a jigsaw puzzle. These all need to come together to allow a complete picture. That is why, if a patient is in hospital with a known psychotic illness, all the involved parties must meet and work together in the patient's interest.

The ward has two functions here: to be a safe container for disturbed behaviour and to provide the setting for further assessment of dangerousness. Ways to optimize the ward's functioning are considered in the final part of this chapter.

The ward setting within an integrated approach

There are three fundamental prerequisites for an effective ward: a good structure, experienced senior nursing staff, and the involvement of a single-sector team. The building has to be appropriate to the purpose of safely containing disturbed behaviour. When we moved our unit from a large asylum to a district setting, my senior nursing staff and I spent much time deciding on and redesigning an old orthopaedic ward. We learned from others' experiences, as we were the last unit to move. The ward was constructed so that male and female sleeping quarters could be kept separate. The daytime rooms were sited at the centre of the ward, providing access for the staff to observe the patients from the nursing station.

When we moved from the asylum, I did my level best to ensure that the team was preserved, with the ward manager and deputy ward manager coming together with as many experienced staff as possible. By relating to a single sector team, we were able to build up a team approach with continuity of care from the hospital to the community. As we know, good communication among the team is of key importance in limiting the risk of tragedy.

Surprisingly, I found that experienced nursing staff did not see violence to themselves from inpatients as their key concern. They seemed to know when they needed to call on the services of the psychiatric intensive care ward. The nurses' main concerns were their managers' reactions to unforeseen events and complaints and the possibility of suspension and disciplinary proceedings. In such circumstances, the support from the consultant is crucial. It helps to foster the open and relaxed atmosphere required by the nature of the work.

Having a good and secure basic setting allows the introduction of analytically informed assessments of dangerousness into the ward round reviews. In Finland, Alanen has developed the "need-adapted approach to psychosis" (Alanen, 1997). He describes how therapeutic activities are planned flexibly on an individual basis. Different therapeutic approaches complement each other, and treatment aims to maintain the quality of a continuous process. A consultant supervisory role, incorporating analytic experience, is required for the need adapted evaluations. Within the team, each member is encouraged to develop his own skills in a creative way. Caring family members or partners play a crucial role in the initial assessments, and they remain involved in the process.

In order to adapt the Scandinavian model to other settings, Alanen emphasized the need for the catchment-area model, with close cooperation between in-patient and out-patient care, access to

a day hospital, supervised residential settings, and an acute psychosis community team.

We have been employing such an approach since the closure of
the asylum, when the move to a district allowed the setting up of a
sector team. A nurse recently described how, with pressure on
beds, the "revolving-door syndrome" has now become more that
of a "cat flap"! Murray Jackson has criticized the "fast-food",
quick-fix attitude of the physical approach that threatens to domi-
nate psychiatry (Jackson, 1997). The pressure to create beds
through early discharge could lead to under-appreciation of the
potential for further violence in an individual patient. The author
has found that an approach in which there is an integration of
analytic understanding and three times weekly ward reviews has
led to shorter stays in hospital, while allowing for full debate and
consideration of the risk of further violence.

The following might serve as an illustrative vignette.

"Mr D"

A young man from an Eastern culture was admitted in an
excitable, grandiose state, having smashed up his home prior to
admission. He said that he was Edward, son of Henry the
Eighth! When I asked him about the delusion, he had no
thoughts or associations to it.

The following day, he was reported to be going around the
ward, asking nurses for a cigar. In my exasperation at the
failure to engage him about his delusion, I said jokingly, "Since
you are Edward, son of Henry the Eighth, you cannot have a
cigar, as they were not introduced until your sister Elizabeth
was on the throne!" The humour was quite lost on him.

Over the next few days, we started on the ward rounds to
discuss and to think collectively about the case. Our social
worker found out that the patient had married a young woman,
and they had a child. It was an arranged marriage to which she
had consented in order to stay in the country. He had been very
grandiose and contemptuous towards her, battering her quite
severely, and she and the baby were currently in a refuge.

When confronted with these details, he denied all the history, simply saying that there was an accommodation problem and that his wife would come back once it had been sorted out. In fact, the initial feedback was that his wife did intend this, because of the fear of deportation. As we started to consider the background situation in greater depth, I was stimulated to think of the meaning of the delusion in terms of an ideograph (Bion, 1957). In Bion's terms, the patient had stored in his mind the memory or ideograph of Edward, son of Henry the Eighth, for a specific purpose. It was to be used to evacuate thoughts arrived at through the functioning of the non-psychotic part of his personality. These thoughts were critical of his psychotic parts: manic, grandiose, aggressively dismissive behaviour towards his wife. This in-touch part had to be disowned.

It occurred to me then that Henry had many wives and treated them as he liked, but he also created his own religion and rules. The patient disowned and displaced into the ideograph his awareness of behaving like the son of such a person, hence creating the delusion. When I tried to discuss this with him, he turned all observations into logical facts, arguing that he came from a different religious background.

However, curiosity about a delusion and about why it is needed can lead to building a link, over time, to the patient's own anxieties about the powerfulness of his psychotic part. The insight can be shared with others involved in the patient's problematic states of mind and their management, hopefully adding depth and interest to their work. This approach contrasts in style with behavioural approaches to delusional material, which advocate reasoned debate, reality-testing experiments, and distancing and distraction if the delusions are too intrusive.

Nevertheless, in spite of all endeavours to communicate fully within the team, unforeseen tragedies will continue to happen. In such situations, it is then important that the nursing staff are supported by their medical colleagues and that the administration does not over-react. The bottom line is that the team has to be kept intact and in a healthy state of morale if it is to continue to function effectively.

CHAPTER FOUR

The psychodynamic assessment of violence in the general medical hospital, or, taking the "non-body" seriously

John Lowe

Modern medicine can be looked upon as a kind of religion of the body. Its multifarious texts and rituals, enacted in its hospital temples, erect a certain ideal of the body—a totem, if you like—onto which real bodies can then be mapped. The medical mission is, then, to purify those actual bodies it meets (known as patients) of all that is deemed foreign or disruptive (known as disease) as measured against that ideal—and, of course, in the process to relieve suffering. But this has not always been the case. For the medieval physician, for example, it was the soul that needed saving not the soma; medicine addressed a very different kind of problematic (Rawcliffe, 2000). In modern times, the idea of medicine as body-centred has emerged and been pursued most fervently and most literally in terms of the anatomical body. Thus, it is still the case that in many institutions the medical student is initiated into his or her chosen profession primarily through an encounter with the body as anatomy—that is, through the dissection of the dead body or cadaver. It hardly needs saying that the choice of the cadaver is no accidental selection from among any number of possible examples of the body—kinetic, mental, social, biochemical, physiological, and so on. This act establishes the medical body as, first and foremost, anatomical. Located and bound up with this is, I believe, a whole set of cultural articulations—mostly unspoken, but perhaps therefore all the more forcefully conveyed—which relate to the reproduction of a particular kind of doctor–patient relationship (Jordanova, 1999). After all, the anatomical body of the mortuary slab is supine, inviting the student to lay open the dark secrets within. It offers no resistance, no movement, no volition, no personality, and no history. In short, this body presents no impediment to the medical gaze. Is it too far-fetched to suggest that recent public controversies over the alleged arrogance of doctors are due at least in part to a conflict over the very idea of the medical body as anatomy? Interestingly, the first drawings of modern anatomical bodies, emerging in Italy in the fifteenth century, did display the human "soul" as well as the bodily sinew; typically cadavers were portrayed in naturalistic and suitably melancholic poses, which reflected their origins—invariably the executioner's scaffold (Kemp & Wallace, 2000). The philosopher and historian Michael Foucault has put the argument in this way:

> For us, the Body defines, by natural right, the space of origin and of distribution of disease: a space whose lines, volumes, surfaces, origins, and routes are laid down, in accordance with a now familiar geometry, by the *anatomical atlas*. But this order of the solid, visible body is only one way—in all likelihood, neither the first, nor the most fundamental—in which one spatializes disease. There have been, and will be, other distributions of illness. [Foucault, 1976, p. 3; emphasis added]

Violence—at least in its physical aspects—is also an encounter with the body. However, the violent body is quite unlike its modern medical counterpart. Violent bodies are not yielding or supine: on the contrary, they are actively resistant. Moreover, to state the obvious, they are not dead. Rather, they are mindful, living organisms intent, for reasons that may or may not be clear, on visiting harm on others or themselves. Therefore the incursion of the potentially violent body into the mental space of the medical hospital is in a way already an act of violence. Insofar as its very presence threatens the central medical idea of the body as submissive, material and definitively knowable, the violent body wreaks havoc with the medical norm. In fact, within the general medical hospital the violent body is typically experienced by doctors, nurses, and others as a *non-body*, which is therefore "nothing to do with us" and so not a suitable subject for medicine. On the other hand, the violent body is, by its very nature, difficult to ignore: it demands to be noticed. Such a body is often labelled "psychiatric" or "difficult" or "personality-disordered" as a prelude to its disposal by various means. This is not to say that such labels are inaccurate or wrong, but, rather, that they tend to be used in a way that is circular and preemptive. It is against this particular institutional background and conflict that the psychodynamic assessment of violence in the general hospital must take place, if it is to take place at all, and why I have termed it "taking the non-body seriously".

It is also in relation to the question of the non-body that the term "psychodynamic" takes on particular significance and force. The non-body viewed in a limited way—say, as a set of faculties of the mind—is much less of an irritant to the conventional medical discourse. As such, the non-body or mind can quite easily be incorporated as a mere epiphenomenon of the body. Thus, for example, the depression that not uncommonly follows a stroke can be understood, in strictly bodily terms, as being due to tissue damage to the brain. Similarly, violence when it occurs can be reduced to biological categories such as metabolism and genetics. Again, this is not to say that such inferences are untrue or without merit, but only to point out that they restrict the domain of enquiry. However, if following Freud we take up the psychodynamic gauntlet then this implies a radical opening up of thought to include the possibility, not just of mind and mindedness, but of unconscious motivation and desire (Freud, 1910a [1909]). Beyond Freud, the term "psychodynamic" suggests the whole web of social meanings, conscious and unconscious, that constitutes the lived experience of both the individuals and the institutions in which they collectively participate. It implies processes and values of understanding and sharing that cannot be either reduced or commuted to the notion of a "cure" from bodily ills. Moreover, an emphasis on attention to social meanings also enables a certain degree of self-reflexiveness, so that a "psychodynamic assessment" is not simply about applying a set of procedures to a given problem, but also involves a consideration of how such an assessment, including the assessor, may become implicated in the difficulty as a *creative act*. In effect, the term psychodynamic implies an altogether different approach to the "business as usual" version of contemporary anatomical medicine; it suggests the primacy of the non-body in an essentially multi-centred interconnected universe, and with that comes a radical re-spatialization of the concept of disease.

Likewise, the use of the adjective "psychodynamic" threatens to explode the meanings of the term "risk" to include the domains of mind and culture. Of course, the idea of potential damage to an underlying psychological structure is implicit in the psychoanalytic theories that inform a psychodynamic approach. And, increasingly, notions of psychological damage, such as post-traumatic stress disorder (PTSD), are now more widely and seriously entertained than ever before. Moreover, the use of the term "psychodynamic" in the sense of an interaction between two or more minds suggests that we should further incorporate into the idea of "risk" the possibility of any social harm that might result from actions intended to reduce the risk of physical hazards—for example, the social alienation that might be consequent upon the chemical sedation or physical restraint of a disturbed patient in the general medical hospital. Once again, this confronts the physician, steeped in the ideology and practice of the body, with the potentially confounding domain of the non-body. Viewed in this way, a competent assessment of violence can no longer be so easily reduced to a question of the numerical probability for a physically violent outcome. Rather, the risk of physical harm needs to be balanced against the risk of social and psychological harm for the same set of proposed circumstances or courses of action. This requires a complex comparison of probabilities between domains—physical, psychological and social—that cannot sensibly be reduced to a single objective axis or dimension. Thus conceived, risk assessment acquires a distinctly qualitative and contextual character that, rather reassuringly is of the kind more familiar to the traditional bedside clinician than to the insurance loss adjuster.

Desecration of the body:
"Mr E"

A young man, Mr E, was brought to casualty having overdosed on intravenous opiates. He had been found collapsed in a nearby fast-food-store toilet. Fortunately, the crash team were able to revive him. However, the patient seemed less than grateful to find himself alive. Accordingly, the casualty staff asked for the opinion of the on-call psychiatrist. In the meantime the patient angrily demanded and received the return of his belongings, including a bottle of antidepressants. The psychiatrist arrived to find the patient in the toilet of the casualty department. The patient subsequently emerged, smiled, and reluctantly agreed to be interviewed. During the course of the interview he became increasingly drowsy, and eventually he admitted that he had taken another overdose—this time of the antidepressants that had been returned to him. This required further medical treatment.

The incursion of the non-body into the hospital as an act of violence perpetrated by the patient on his own body is far from unusual. Indeed, deliberate self harm is the most common cause of admission to the general medical hospital for women of working age, and the second-highest-ranking cause of death of men under the age of 35 (Hawton et al., 1998). Research shows that with appropriate training non-psychiatric casualty staff are able to effectively and safely manage presentations of deliberate self-harm. Moreover, a number of interventions may well have a preventative value. It would be entirely reasonable to pick up the discussion of the above case in such terms—namely, the ubiquity of such cases and the need for improved resources for assessment and treatment. Alternatively, one could use such a case as a springboard for constructing a set of clinical practice guidelines that might be applied with good effect in similar cases. Either response would be a legitimate and potentially helpful action to take. However, this would not amount to a psychodynamic appreciation of the case material or of the clinical situation. Such an approach would insist on a series of questions that place us firmly in the realm of the non-body, such as why did this man try to harm himself? What were his reasons?

Why were his tablets returned to him, enabling him take a second overdose? Clearly, we may or may not be able to provide satisfactory answers to such questions, let alone guarantee a translation into concrete action. However, in a sense such questions are already posed by the act of self harm itself—they seem to almost "hang in the air" whenever a case like this presents. In other words, these appear to be questions of meaning that are demanded by the dynamics of the situation itself, which capture our interest at the outset and continue to drive our search for "solutions".

Turning to the case itself, it is of course difficult to be conclusive, given the scant detail available. However, this would not be untypical. The clinician must, as ever, work with what is to hand. Moreover, as I indicated earlier, a psychodynamic assessment conducted in terms of the elucidation of meaning cannot, however comprehensive the information available, produce a final answer in the way that, say, a blood result can. Rather, assessment in the realm of the non-body—as opposed to the physical and factual world of the body—deals with social and psychic meanings which, while not wholly independent of the "facts" and certain cultural "rules", are also crucially governed by the individual assessors professional predilections and flair. What strikes me most about cases such as this is what I term the desecration of the body. This case in particular, I think, highlights the patient's determination to attack his own body even in the very Temple of the Body—namely, the hospital itself. In the process the hospital is satirized in a cruel and rather desperate way; it is recast as a site for a ritual of contamination rather than one of cleansing. Understandably, medical staff tend to blind themselves to such unsavoury non-body possibilities. Of course, during the period of an acute medical crisis this is often very necessary in order that all efforts can be directed towards saving the actual body and with it the potential for life in the patient. However, once the body has been saved, as in this case, it is not unusual for that blinding to persist—partly, I think, in order to protect the patient from the hate that such knowledge might unleash, and partly to spare the staff members themselves the discomfort of such hate. Of course the unconscious existence of such resentment, as well as the conscious ignorance, is doubtless betrayed in this case at the point at which the tablets were handed back by the staff to the patient. Through this act it is possible to see the outline of a wish to punish or rid oneself altogether of this particular medical tormentor, this despoiler of the body. In his classic essay "The Ailment", Tom Main makes a similar point, both succinctly and powerfully: "The sufferer who frustrates a keen therapist by failing to improve is always in danger of meeting primitive human behaviour disguised as treatment" (Main, 1957, p. 129).

In the general medical hospital it is not just a simple "failure to improve" that elicits primitive and defensive responses, but also the intrusion of the non-body into the domain and discourse of the medical and medicalized body.

Control of the body:
"Mrs F"

Mrs F, a woman in her thirties with renal failure, suffered a serious complication of peritoneal dialysis. This resulted in a fibrosis of the membranes of her gut, which meant that she was unable to take nutrition enterally—that is, by mouth. Instead, she required Total Parenteral Nutrition (TPN), consisting of liquid given intravenously. The outlook for her condition was extremely poor, and Mrs F was not expected to survive for more than a year. The patient was married, with two young children. Understandably, staff found it difficult to discuss how bleak the situation was with the patient herself. After some weeks of her TPN regime, the patient began to refuse her treatment. It was felt by ward staff that Mrs F might be depressed, and a referral was made to the liaison psychiatrist. However, although the psychiatrist found that Mrs F was understandably sad and unhappy, he did not feel that she had mental health problems. Rather, it seemed to him that the patient had made a decision not to continue with a treatment that she loathed and which, she knew, could not save her. In effect, she had made a decision to take control of her own death and to end her suffering sooner rather than later. Initially, staff found this very hard to accept. One member of the ward staff asked the psychiatrist if there was any way in which the patient could be "forced" to accept treatment. It was explained that in the circumstances this was not possible. Ultimately, with the support of the psychiatrist, staff were able to accept the patient's decision to take control of her own body in this way and to feel good about the care that they had provided for her. However, they would never allow the patient's death to be referred to as a "suicide"—that is, a deliberate killing of one's own body and self.

The dying patient presents particular emotional difficulties to any professional carer, especially when the illness is in part a consequence of treatment. The wish to repair and heal is all the more intense if a portion of the damage has been inflicted by the carers themselves. When under these circumstances the patient refuses to comply with the treatment being proposed—that is, to allow the doctor or the nurse free access to the body—then further difficulties can arise. In this case staff had already turned a blind eye to the body rather than the non-body of the patient inasmuch as they had disavowed the true nature of that body—namely, that it was a dying body. There appeared to be a kind of institutional denial of the real nature of the illness, which allowed the staff to cling on to a hope of cure and to avoid the despair and guilt that otherwise they would surely feel. Of course, the poor communication with the patient about her prognosis fed into this denial. However, it seems likely that somehow the "bad news" was communicated unconsciously to the patient, who as a consequence quite reasonably decided that it was time to face up to her death. To do this, she needed to take her body into her own hands, so to speak. This provoked quite a hostile reaction from some of the staff, who felt frightened by the reality of this patient's impending death and also affronted by her wilful actions. Initially, they preferred to see her as a "difficult" or "depressed" patient who needed to be brought back into line in some way. Doubtless, the resultant impasse between patient and staff, which prevailed for a time, also diverted attention for both parties away from the real issue: namely, the fact that a married woman with children was about to die partly due to an adverse reaction to treatment, and that there was nothing that could be done to change that fact.

In a sense, this example illustrates how the psychodynamic assessment of a situation such as this needs to take into account not just the non-body of the patient but also the professional non-body of the staff—that is, the difficult non-professional feelings that all carers experience when the care of the patient fails in some way. Those feelings—largely of guilt and fear—in this example were initially evaded by a collective denial of the parlous state of the patient's body and the reasons for its decline. Subsequently, when by her "non-compliant" actions the patient insisted on her sovereignty over her dying body, staff felt threatened and sought to project their own uncomfortable feelings into the patient by denying her reality and casting her as "depressed" or "difficult". Accepting those feelings back is, of course, never easy. In fact, it was the staff and not the patient who were struggling with the non-bodily parts of themselves, and it was they and not Mrs F who needed psychological support. Once that had been given, staff were then able to return to the job of looking after the actual body of their patient. However, they still found it difficult to accept fully that with the acquiescence of staff the patient had in fact willed her own death while she was a patient on the ward.

Hatred of the body:
"Mr G"

Mr G, a 65-year-old West Indian man with diabetes, obesity, heart failure, and renal failure, who was on the renal transplant waiting list, was upset to learn that after several years of waiting for a suitable donor kidney, one had still not been found for him. He understood that because of his age and other medical conditions, younger and fitter patients would be likely to get more benefit with less risk from a transplantation procedure and therefore had higher priority. He knew that donor organs were scarce. In the meantime he continued to receive treatment in the form of peritoneal dialysis. However, he became increasingly convinced that he was being unfairly treated because of his African origins and ethnicity. In particular, he was sure that the transplant coordinator, an Asian woman in her thirties, was conducting a personal vendetta against him. He wrote many letters of complaint to the transplant coordinator, and on several occasions was verbally abusive and physically threatening towards her. Mr G was referred to the psychiatrist for an assessment. Not surprisingly, he was reluctant to see the psychiatrist, but eventually he did agree to do so. It emerged that

Mr G was quite convinced that the transplant coordinator wished him ill for some reason, perhaps because of his colour. In fact, he believed that she used magic or witchcraft to turn others against him, to read his thoughts, and to poison his blood. It also transpired that Mr G was in many ways a disappointed and lonely man, who had emigrated from Trinidad in the 1960s with great hopes for his future, only to find himself in low-paid menial work and the victim on several occasions of racial abuse and attack. His wife had died several years previously, and he had no children.

It is not hard to sympathize with Mr G's situation and plight. His age and poor physical health mean that in a world where resources and donor organs are scarce, his chances of a successful transplant were probably never very good. Moreover, his experiences of discrimination as a black immigrant, his childlessness, and the loss of his wife make his resentment and anger all the more understandable. However, it seems that more than this is at issue here. It would appear that Mr G attached his anger in a rather bizarre albeit culturally inflected way to one particular individual, the transplant coordinator. It is as if he holds her responsible for all his troubles, inasmuch as she is, he believes, unjustly withholding that which would restore his health and contentment—namely, a donor kidney. The loathing and hate that Mr G feels for his misfortunes, society, and body appear to have been located in the person—or, more specifically, the non-bodily intent—of a female carer. What is also apparent is the "magical" thought processes that have linked the alleged perpetrator to Mr G's grievances. It is as though the figure of the transplant coordinator has become in Mr G's mind a monstrous maternal presence that threatens to engulf and take over the self—hence her capacity to read Mr G's thoughts.

Following the work of Melanie Klein and the British object relations theorists we might see this case an example of what can happen when the individual's internal sense of security is overwhelmed (Klein, 1960). When faced with such overwhelming adversity, Mr G's internal mother was no longer able to, so to speak, mop up all his hate and anger. Instead, this internal object relationship broke down into a much more primitive, fragmented, and malevolent form in which the transplant coordinator was identified as a bad mother figure. Presumably, this allowed Mr G to retain for himself some sense of a good internal mother and some security within, but at the price of a key external relationship. Mr G's feelings of betrayal, both by his own body and by the social body of the society in which he dwelt, had in his fantasy been lodged in, but not contained by, the person of his carer.

Concluding remarks

The general medical hospital is not typically associated with the act of violence, in spite of the fact that medicine is still often a bloody and painful affair in which minds and bodies are torn apart by disease and sometimes by the very treatments that aim to cure. But the violence of the doctor and his or her treatment is sanctioned because it is predicated on the intention to cure or palliate, and because it is presumed to be exercised with care and skill. Consonant with this, the medical tradition has tended to locate knowledge and volition with the doctor rather than the patient. In the process, the patient has occupied the position of the body—supine and pliable—and the doctor the place of the non-body or sovereign self. Arguably, in the normal course of events this may not be important; however, as I have tried to show, there are situations where this split between body and non-body, patient and doctor, can have substantive consequences that need to be addressed and, if at all possible, understood. In particular, in certain situations where patients express a violent agency either directly or indirectly, there may be a failure of recognition on the part of medical staff.

To understand this collective medical "blind eye" would itself require a psychodynamic assessment, albeit of an historical variety. Clearly, it may have something to do with the timeless needs of those who enter the caring professions to "take charge" of other people and situations as a proxy for their own internal "demons". However, this would not by itself explain the peculiarly bodily form that such a need for control has assumed in our own era. It seems to me that a fuller understanding of such a phenomenon would require an appreciation of a range of political and social factors and their historical development—for example, the rise of the "teaching hospital" and of "medicine as a profession". However, that has not been my task here. Rather, I was concerned to elucidate some of the more characteristic medical scenarios in which patients not infrequently act as agents or mediators of violence, usually against their own bodies, often—but not always—with the aim of attacking either the minds and capacities of their carers or their own non-bodily functions. I wanted to show how such "offers"—to use a term favoured by Balint (1957)—are generally received and greeted in the medical environment. Characteristically, this reception is based on an organized, albeit unconscious, misunderstanding that arises out of a need not to "see" the message that the patient is attempting, also unconsciously, to communicate. This failure to "see", at least at a conscious level, may play into the symptomatic structures of the patient's disturbance, leading to a repetition or even escalation of the violent interplay. The psychodynamic assessment of violence in the general medical hospital is, therefore, an essential starting point for an effective intervention in this kind of case. How such an assessment can be turned into an effective intervention in this particular kind of environment is, of course, a subject all its own.

CHAPTER FIVE

Psychoanalytic aspects to the risk containment of dangerous patients treated in high-security hospital

Carine Minne

The perplexing or shocking behaviours that can lead patients, psychotic or otherwise, to be treated in secure settings may have contributed to the tendency of forensic psychiatry teams in particular to incorporate a psychoanalytic approach. In addition, psychoanalytic thinking is considered helpful with those patients suffering from personality disorders for whom "ordinary" psychiatric management does not seem to suffice. In this chapter, I first describe in a general way how clinical psychiatric teams in high-secure hospital settings approach the problem of patients who have been violent. I then give examples of "dangerous" patients who have been treated with psychoanalytic psychotherapy and show how this approach can contribute to understanding their difficulties and violent propensities, adding an important aspect to their management.

Patients in special hospital or high security are, by definition, considered to be "dangerous". This means that a particular individual, who has committed violent acts in the past is likely to behave violently again. "Violence" in psychiatric literature is widely accepted to be "the intended infliction of bodily harm on another person", and this definition requires there to be a breach in body boundary (Glasser, 1996, 1998). The first difficulty immediately apparent from a psychoanalytic perspective is that the description refers to the quality of an individual's previous actions rather than saying anything about the individual himself (Mullen, 1984). This causes a pull towards a behavioural approach in examining the problem, because violent acts can be seen and measured. However, this approach alone does not suffice, and the simple fact that a previously violent person has not been violent for a certain amount of time—maybe for years—does not tell us anything about the likelihood of future violent behaviour. Neither does it provide any understanding of the meaning of the violence committed. A multifactorial perspective is therefore necessary in order to arrive at meaningful clinical appraisals. A psychoanalytic approach can contribute by offering a view of the patient's mind and how his or her past dangerous behaviour resides in that mind. Psychoanalytic theories are also useful in the quest to understand why certain patients who suffer from mental disorders appear to have inadequate defences against the discharge of violent impulses. One should not forget that, along with environmental contributing factors, constitutional features can also play a role.

A history of previous violence is considered to be the best predictor of future violence for all people, mentally disordered or not. Simply keeping patients locked up indefinitely, apart from being unethical, ignores the multifaceted nature of dangerousness, the temporal dimension, and the existence of treatments that can be offered to those with mental disorders. It also implies that society believes it can rid itself of a problem, that only revenge matters, or that if there is any hope of effective treatments, these are not deserved. Such primitive "tabloid" ways of dealing with these complex issues are inhumane, short-sighted, and, just like the problem behaviours these patients present with, mindless. One task for the clinical team, and perhaps in particular, the psychoanalytic psychotherapist, is to help the patient begin to "mind" what they have previously had to keep "mindless". Nevertheless, it is important to consider the public perception of mentally disordered offenders and how this influences policy-makers, particularly those involved with the high-secure hospital patient population. It should be considered a duty of those professionals involved in treating this patient population to have an input in policy-making.

The three Special Hospitals in England and Wales (Broadmoor, Rampton, and Ashworth) provide psychiatric care under conditions of high security for patients who must pose *a grave and immediate risk*. These hospitals house approximately 1,500 patients who are detained under the 1983 Mental Health Act (mainly under sections in Part 3 of that Act, which deals with patients concerned in criminal proceedings), which was reviewed with the Mental Health White Paper, December 2000. The second part of this White Paper addresses the "high-risk patients" and outlines new criteria that would link compulsory powers with the treatment plans needed to treat mental disorders or to manage behaviours arising from the disorders. This part of the White Paper also refers to the proposed establishing of new facilities for those who are dangerous and severely personality disordered (DSPD), about which there is a great deal of controversy.

Most patients in high security are considered dangerous only some of the time and only when certain ingredients come together. It is another task of the clinical team to review these ingredients or factors continuously. The term "risk containment" (Monahan, 1993) is used to describe the multifaceted approach required when considering a patient who has been dangerous. Snowden (1997) has provided a helpful way of considering risk containment under three broad headings.

1. *Risk identification:*   What is the nature of the risk being considered? Is it a risk of harm towards the self or of violent behaviour towards others? Is the risk one of relapse of a particular mental illness that is known to be associated with violence?

2. *Frequency and severity:*   The identified risk is assessed in terms of the frequency with which it might recur and the probable severity of any recurrence. As much information as possible should be obtained about the patient's background and past, including previous and present behaviour as well as previous and present mental states. All possible sources of information, ranging from old school reports, police records or social-work reports, to conversations with relatives or neighbours, should

be sought by the different professionals in the clinical team. This enables a thorough appraisal of as many facets as possible of a particular patient, leading to the best-informed clinical judgement when assessing the risk.

3. *Clinical risk management:*   Treating the patient's mental disorder by providing multidisciplinary input that helps to reduce the frequency and severity of the identified and assessed risks. One form of treatment, directly or indirectly applied, is psychoanalytic psychotherapy. A long-term aim is to enable patients to "contain" themselves.

The level of dangerousness of any patient in high-secure conditions can vary from day to day and has to be assessed repeatedly to ensure that they receive the most effective treatments available. It also allows evaluation of the appropriate level of observation and security and ensures that, when the patient is ready to move to less secure conditions, this is judged thoughtfully on clinical grounds.

Looking at it from the perspective of the whole institution, risk containment for each individual case should be systematically reviewed and revised in the light of regular clinical auditing and research. Risk containment can then, hopefully, become more refined and continue to develop to benefit patients, those looking after them, and society. All these aspects of a patient's management also form part of the wider rubric of the Care Programme Approach, which must be applied to every patient suffering from mental disorder to ensure that they get the full care and support they need once they are back in the community.

How does a person become a Special Hospital patient? The patients in high security may come directly from the courts when a hospital order has been imposed on them; they may also be transferred from prison while on remand for assessment or treatment, or they may have become ill while serving a sentence; they may also be transferred from less secure hospital conditions if their management there has become problematic. It is certainly worth bearing in mind that approximately one third of the sentenced prison population in England and Wales (now over 60,000) is estimated to suffer from some kind of mental disorder (Gunn & Maden, 1993). Several hundred of these people require secure hospital treatment, which cannot be provided adequately because of a shortage of facilities. It is mainly long-stay medium-secure hospital beds that are desperately needed.

It constitutes a misperception that people in high secure hospital conditions are frequently referred to as prisoners or inmates. They have certainly lost their freedom, but they are patients who are in hospital to receive treatment. The move to calling them "prisoners" represents the familiar pull towards a custodial and punitive focus and away from the idea of treatment, often misconstrued by the general public as condoning the awful offences that have been committed. What is required is the right balance for each individual case between the positions of treatment provided by the mental health professionals, and punishment plus loss of freedom provided, respectively, by the Criminal Justice System and the secure environment. Both are essential for the proper care of any patient and the safety of the public. The difficulties in achieving this balance contribute to the particular dynamics of working under conditions of high security, where the demands of treatment and security can seem to clash.

For example, all those working in Special Hospitals carry, tied to their waists, an enormous bunch of keys, and the impact of this cannot be ignored. It emphasizes a "them versus us" scenario: the envious versus the enviable. Here, straight away, a most concrete split is set up: patients and professionals are, as it were, dressed in their respective costumes, ready to enact the familiar sado-masochistic script so often apparent in situations where dangerous or "bad" people are housed. Unless one remains constantly aware of this, one can easily fall prey to the magnetic pull of such transference and countertransference phenomena and find oneself again and again colluding in an enactment of the patient's internal world. In such institutions, primitive communications fly around in all directions, since patients with these levels of disturbance have a special expertise in projecting all over the place and into every available container. The nurses have the most difficult task of all in these hospitals: as they are with the patients 24 hours a day, they are the main recipients of these projections. However, this does at the same time place the nurses in a particularly valuable position for monitoring the patients' states of mind and contributing towards the assessment of dangerousness, which, as stated earlier, needs to be a continuous part of the risk-containment of these patients.

How can a forensic psychoanalytic psychotherapist come into the picture and offer another dimension in the risk containment strategy? Working directly with patients in therapy offers an opportunity for regular reviews of patients' mental states while working therapeutically. Alternatively, psychotherapists can work indirectly, through supervising other professionals treating these patients in therapy or by being available to speak to primary nurses (each patient is allocated his or her own main or primary nurse) about their patients in the hope of offering them another way of speaking and listening to their patients. Ward rounds and case conferences are also settings in which the presence of the forensic psychoanalytic psychotherapist can be useful—for example, by helping a team that has become divided about how a particular patient should best be managed. The aim in all of these situations is to improve the awareness of the unconscious processes at work. Increased understanding of the unconscious processes in a patient's mind and, consequently, in his or her interactions can add an invaluable dimension to risk assessment. Providing psychoanalytic therapeutic treatment as part of the overall care plan can also contribute to the "risk containment" of a particular case.

It is one major task of this kind of psychotherapy to enable awareness of the mind and its functions to become available to the owner of that mind—the patient. This includes an awareness of who he is, what he has done, and the impact of this on his mind and on the minds of others—that is, making what is unconscious conscious. Often patients who have carried out serious violent offences demonstrate a high degree of unawareness, regardless of their diagnosis. This can manifest itself in various ways, such as denial, disavowal, minimization, and amnesia. This lack of awareness can appear to be necessary for the patient's psychic survival. If they relinquish "not knowing", they may then become overwhelmed by the knowledge of who they are and what they have done. This can cause massive anxieties about "cracking up" and can lead to psychotic breakdowns (if they are not already manifestly psychiatrically psychotic) and, perhaps, to suicide. The therapist's task is therefore a delicate and complicated one. They must (1) help the cultivation of awareness in the patient's mind without seeming to commit a violent assault on that person's internal world, (2) judge whether such awareness is developing, and (3) understand in what way this is being used by the patient. Experience has shown that any such achievements by patient and therapist together can function, at an unconscious level, as a provocation of a part of a patient's mind that envies the successful union of patient and therapist and aim to destroy it through denigration of the work done.

A psychotherapist working in these situations has to achieve a difficult balance—namely, confidentiality for the patient versus the need to communicate information if and when issues of security or risk arise. This is something that has to be reviewed every time a situation of this kind comes up. As a psychoanalytic psychotherapist, one tries to offer patients confidentiality for obvious therapeutic reasons. One might perhaps facilitate a patient's informing the clinical team of a change in risk, for example, in dangerousness towards self or another. However, this is sometimes not possible, and then one has to assess how best to proceed. There may be a need to communicate something directly to the clinical team, although this should be discussed with the patient. I have found that patients are often relieved to be helped in informing the team of a change in risk. They may also be relieved if I do this for them, even though their getting me to "do" something has then to be interpreted. Disclosure by the patient, or by the therapist on behalf of the patient, can itself result in a diminution of the risk by virtue of the patient having felt understood. One of the striking differences between forensic psychotherapy and psychotherapy generally is the presence of a real third object creating a triangular situation (Welldon, 1994).

This way of working can be illustrated using some examples of patients in high-security hospitals who have had psychoanalytic psychotherapy as part of their treatment plan. There are, of course, many other examples of patients who have not had individual psychoanalytic psychotherapy but with whom a psychoanalytic approach has been used in assessing and treating. This is more often the case with high-security patients, since only a few can be offered individual therapy of this kind at present. Many patients are in psychoanalytic psychotherapy groups or are treated by a clinical team that uses psychoanalytically informed thinking.

"Mr H"

Mr H is 24 years old and was admitted to a high-security hospital when a court imposed a hospital order with a Home Office restriction at the conclusion of his trial. He had been convicted of murder. The offence for which he was arrested occurred in a public place late one evening when no one other than his female victim was around. He carried out what appeared to be an impulsive, unprovoked, and extremely serious attack on a woman using a sharp weapon, leaving her fatally injured. He ran away before giving himself up to the police. He had no prior record of violent offences. He did not appear overtly mentally disordered, but his vulnerability and neediness were soon detected while he was on remand in prison, and this, combined with his young age, led to psychiatric reports being requested for his trial.

At first, Mr H's offence was described by him as a one-off event, a handbag theft that had gone wrong. However, the extreme violence that he had used, attacking this woman with the full strength of his body, was not in keeping with this explanation, and it was considered early on that, psychically, a different scenario may have been acted out. After several months in hospital, he admitted this. This had been a conscious withholding on his part of what he thought he knew about his action, as opposed to any unconscious denial.

He started psychoanalytic psychotherapy shortly after his admission to high security. He pleaded to have this and, as soon as it was offered, began to use the sessions to complain about how little had been provided compared with what he needed. He said that he wanted, and should have, someone available to talk to 24 hours a day, someone who would provide continuous unconditional care. His mother had in fact left the family home with a lover when his younger sibling was born, leaving her husband to look after a 3-year-old toddler, Mr H, and a new-born baby. It was not difficult to piece together that, as a very young child, Mr H had suffered a major trauma, which had led to unprocessed grief for his enormous early loss. This loss, perhaps in combination with his particular constitution, may have caused his mind to fill with unbearable feelings of rage, which he had to get rid of. Around the age of 4 years, he began to make Plasticine models with violent themes—figurines attacking each other with weapons. This was apparently a preoccupation beyond the ordinary limits of a little boy's play. He also started to behave aggressively towards little children who seemed to have "nice mummies" bringing them to school. He was clearly a very troubled child, furiously unhappy at his abandonment, the cause of which appeared to be the arrival of a baby girl, who displaced not only him but also his mother. Sadly, these early manifestations of his disturbance, which were in fact noticed by parental figures and teachers, were addressed unhelpfully. He was simply reprimanded for making and doing ugly things.

With the onset of puberty, Mr H's unresolved rage became attached to his developing sexual feelings. He began to masturbate to fantasies of rape and strangulation. This evolved into stalking women, and several times he came close to attacking a particular woman he had been following, only to "chicken out" at the last moment, leaving the woman totally unaware of what had nearly happened to her. The eventual victim was not so fortunate. What was presented initially by him as a robbery that went wrong could later be seen in quite a different light, as an apparently impulsive attack which had actually been premeditated and rehearsed over a long period of time. There had therefore been an ominous escalation in his dangerousness from fantasy only, to practising carrying these out, and finally, to an incomplete enactment of his main fantasy.

Here we can see how the capacity to symbolize (through fantasies) gradually breaks down as the severity of the psychotic functioning increases. Anxiety is engendered by the very fantasies that are created in order to resolve it, and this fuels the escalation until the fantasies no longer suffice and a deterioration into action is required.

This is a young man whose early feelings of rage at the loss of his mother threaten to overwhelm his psyche. He therefore has to get rid of these in the only way he can, by projecting them violently into a recipient who fulfils his unconscious criteria. Any woman can be a potential victim if she is experienced by him as ignoring him and behaving as if there is nothing the matter. His female victim, who turned away from facing him, could therefore be said to represent the mother who turns her back on him, but she is also the object of his envy, since she is free of the disturbance he is experiencing. She is also someone who, in his mind, is happily on her way home and therefore has a home to go to, which he does not. At that moment of perceiving the woman, he has to defend against the rage and anxiety that his states of motherlessness and homelessness provoke in him and which, he feels, have been provoked by the object, the woman aggressor. He tries to achieve this by reversing the situation. Instead of feeling at the mercy of a cruel and abandoning object, he attempts to control the object by the attempted rape, which did not happen (but would have been another way of filling the object with his rage) and the killing, which did. One could say that it was not the woman's handbag he was trying to steal but her sense of well-being.

In his therapy, he tries to defend against the perceived attacks on his psyche by presenting himself as knowing exactly what his needs are and demanding that they be met. He cannot be satiated. When he experiences the inevitable frustrations of his unmet demands, or when he discovers that he is not in control of his objects, he becomes furious. This can be triggered by, for example, the therapist saying that the session has ended. The loss of his omnipotent control of his object leads to a fury that knows no solution other than expulsion through violent acting out, hence the need for special safety precautions for patient and therapist around the sessions. This fury was confirmed by the patient, who said he felt like a pressure cooker inside his head and that the pressure was released in the split-second following the attack.

This experience of lack of control of his objects can also get repeated in his therapy, when he occasionally hears me say things that he has not intended me to say: I am not what, and how, he wants me to be. His response in these moments can either be one of fury, when he shouts angrily at me or walks out before "losing it", or, alternatively, he feels he is the victim of my psychic assault on his mind. During these moments Mr H is highly dangerous. In the first situation, his propensity to act violently towards me or somebody else on the ward is massively increased, at least until that particular state of mind has subsided. In the second situation, the risk is more likely to be to himself. While he feels he is the victim, not just of his therapist but of the whole awful world, he could harm himself in order to punish by inducing guilt. He can therefore be identified simultaneously with both aggressor and victim. As his therapist, I can be made to feel very anxious and frightened at those intense moments, and it is important to use those feelings constructively to formulate the best interpretation under the difficult circumstances. It is vital both to acknowledge my fear to myself and to use this to speak to the patient informatively about what he is then doing to me, his object.

Occasionally, this particular patient presents as innocent and harmless. At these moments, the patient is actually sufficiently disturbed to believe he is a nice young man who is misunderstood. It is my view that, at these moments, the patient's belief is of delusional intensity and is not simply an over-valued idea. This presentation can be very convincing as well as alluring, and professionals can find it hard not to be taken in. One way of trying to avoid feeling anxious and frightened while being with such a patient is to collude with the delusion that he is not disturbed. Serious errors of judgement can be made at these moments. Reassuring the patient might well function as a sedative for both patient and therapist but it is a false reassurance for both. These "nice" states are often brittle and can swiftly shift to a more obvious hostile presentation or angry state of mind. For example, this patient has been known to shout at me: "How can you say that? You treat me as if I was a dangerous person!" At this moment, the patient's awareness of who he is and what he has done is not available to him, and the therapist, in order to be of any use to the patient at that moment, has to be prepared to remind him of what he definitely does not want to be reminded of. This can be experienced by the patient as an attempt by the therapist to kill him, albeit psychically, and he may need to defend himself against this. Again it is a moment of increased risk of dangerousness when he might get rid of his feelings by acting them out. The next immediate interpretation therefore needs to be to show the patient how, when he is reminded of who he is, he feels traumatized by this. The hope is that when this has been repeated in therapy hundreds of times, it may gradually become less necessary for this to be a bodily experience of rage and terror for the patient and more able to be experienced in his mind. These moments of increased risk of acting out are therefore diminished in frequency and intensity by the constant working through of the repetitious splits that take place. The therapeutic work attempts to transform the patient from having no awareness of himself and being obliviously at risk of again behaving dangerously, to having awareness of himself and being mentally equipped to be able to deal with the traumatic effect of this knowledge and the despair it can cause.

"Ms K"

Ms K is a 27-year-old woman who killed her 9-week-old daughter and, later, seriously wounded a professional. She comes from a large and highly dysfunctional family where transgenerational incestuous relationships have resulted in no one being sure of who is who in the extended family. Violence between different sets of parents, mother with father and mother with stepfathers, was the norm. There was no experience of consistent mothering. Around puberty this young woman developed a tic disorder which was eventually treated with medication.

She met a young man when she was 19 years old, and she made a conscious decision that he was the man she would leave home for, marry, and have children with. Prior to this, she had had no serious boyfriends, and one could speculate to what extent Ms K was attempting to undo some of the chaos she had been raised in by having a "white wedding". Following their marriage, she and her husband lived with his alcoholic mother.

Ms K was soon delighted to discover that she was pregnant. However, the stress of this event on this ill-equipped young couple led to the breakdown of their marriage late in her pregnancy. She returned home to live with her own mother, but within days of delivering a healthy baby girl her mother asked her to leave and go to live elsewhere. This behaviour was quite typical of this mother, who later, for example, frequently told the patient that she probably would be better off committing suicide than causing all this trouble. Ms K and her new-born baby moved in with a family friend.

Ms K developed concerns about her baby soon after she was born. She was convinced that the baby was sick, and she called her Health Visitor and GP on a regular basis but could never accept reassurance. On one occasion she stated that the baby had started to manifest facial tics like her own, of such severity that the baby's breathing was affected. The mother and baby were admitted to hospital for the baby to be monitored. Initially, the baby was found to be well, but after two days her condition began to deteriorate. No cause for this deterioration could be found. The baby became critically ill and needed to be looked after in intensive care before dying from cardiac and respiratory failure that did not respond to intensive treatment.

Ms K, bereft, went home to her mother. Soon after the baby's death and post-mortem, laboratory reports showed in the baby's blood toxic levels of a particular medication that was considered to have caused death from poisoning. This was the medication Ms K was on for her illness. She was arrested and charged with murdering her baby. In view of her fragile mental state, her remand period was spent in psychiatric hospital. She denied any wrongdoing for over a year, until the end of the trial, when she admitted having given the baby her medication, not to kill the baby but out of concern that the doctors and nurses were not looking after the baby properly. Retrospectively, it could be suggested that her own bad experience of being mothered was projected twice over: once into her own baby, by identifying with her mother, and then again by projective identification with the nurses and doctors, who became the bad parents for not noticing what was going on, either with the actual baby or with Ms K herself—also a sick baby.

She was admitted to medium security on a hospital order from the court, having been finally convicted of manslaughter. She then had to be transferred to high security after seriously wounding a member of staff. She had also become violent towards herself, cutting herself deeply, hanging herself, and making attempts to strangle herself.

Ms K started in psychoanalytic psychotherapy following her transfer to high security. During the first few months of treatment she presented as a model, compliant patient, who did as she imagined was expected of her in that situation, which is no more than one can expect from someone with such a history. She presented as a distressed patient who spoke about what a dreadful thing she had done, but all of this had a "pseudo" feel to it. This way of presenting to me was gradually interpreted as one way she had of avoiding feeling traumatized or victimized by her own disturbed state of mind both at the time of her offences and now in the room with me. This led to suicidality and a further increase in her dangerousness towards herself for a period of time.

In some sessions during these early months of therapy she was more able to speak to me about what she had done to her baby—how she had crushed her tablets and secretly fed this to the baby—over and over again. At these moments, her real distress was very apparent. She described her preoccupation at the time with her belief that the baby was not being looked after properly by the nurses and doctors. I said to her, at these moments in her sessions, that she wished to be the baby that could be looked after properly. This is a highly ambivalent situation for this patient. If she allows herself to be looked after properly, this negates the looking after that took place within her family structure, so if she engages with the therapy, this creates a sense of betraying her family. I had to be kept, therefore, as someone who was bound to harm her in some way, thus re-enacting her history and the offence.

The pathological mother–child dynamic present in this patient's mind also came into her therapy when, unbeknown to anyone, she took an overdose before a session and arrived with glazed eyes and bilateral hand tremor. When her physical state was commented on, she denied several times that anything was the matter, before becoming angry and shouting that there was no point in all this, she wanted to be with her baby. She kept me in a concerned state and, since I thought it likely that she had taken an overdose, I told her that I thought she wanted me to be a good mother and guess what was the matter. This was followed by a long silence. I then said that I believed she would be relieved if I guessed. I proceeded to tell her that I thought she wanted me to know that she had taken an overdose. If I did not notice this, then she could congratulate herself that she was right: no one notices that she is serious about suicide. If I did notice, she would get something from me, but it would feel spoilt because of how she got it. In this situation, the patient did finally admit to having taken an overdose, which then required urgent medical intervention. Again, in this session, the offence is repeated: a baby, herself, is harmed, again with medication, but this time the baby is saved. Indeed, the "being saved" actually led to a manic outburst of profuse thanks, which diluted the seriousness of what had just happened and allowed her to avoid the experience of guilt that such a rescue could provoke. For this patient, committing suicide could also be seen as a re-enactment of her offence by killing her mother's baby.

During the second and third years of the therapy, the patient's mental state gradually altered, vacillating between manic well-being, when she would deny any need of further treatment, and overt hostility towards her therapist who would not collude with her delusion of wellness. The periods of hostility were occasionally very severe, lasting many months. At these times her dangerousness towards her therapist were judged to be high, and special precautions had to be taken. This was a patient who had once seriously wounded a member of staff who told her to put away all the photographs she clung on to of her baby, saying that it was now time to get on with her life. The patient, at that moment, may have perceived that person as telling her to bring to an end her apparent mourning. Again, this is a complicated situation for Ms K. It calls into question both the nature of the attachment to the object that has been harmed and, consequently, the nature of the mourning. During the periods of overt hostility towards her therapist, the patient may have been perceiving the therapist as telling her to continue with the apparent mourning when she wanted to be manically freed of this. Neither of these is a satisfactory position for Ms K's unresolved and complicated state of bereavement. At these moments the patient is a danger to those intimately involved with her—her therapist, the nurses and other professionals closely involved in her care, and also certain patients on the same ward who are known to take on "co-therapist" roles—rather than posing a risk to strangers.

Late in the third year of treatment Ms K's mental state deteriorated into a more overtly psychotic presentation. She appeared perplexed and had paranoid delusions of being poisoned by staff as well as experiencing olfactory and auditory hallucinations. She stopped eating and drinking and required transfer to the medical ward, where she seemed relieved and gratified to be tube-fed. She never refused this; it was as though she was delegating her need to torture herself to those around her, including her therapist. What emerged after several months was a patient who appeared to be depressed and who described suffering a very low mood. She also presented with many of the biological symptoms of depression, as well as prominent psychomotor retardation. She complained of flashbacks and nightmares; the content of these always concerned witnessing her daughter's last hours attached to life-saving equipment and then being in the morgue with a damaged dead body. Many sessions were brief and consisted of the patient slowly shuffling into the room with her head down, making no eye contact, and saying in a monotonous voice: "I can't keep going like this, I want to be with my baby, I can't continue with this therapy, I can't stand the pain, I don't deserve to live, I don't deserve to die, look what I did to my baby, I must suffer for this." She would eventually ask a nurse to come and liberate her from me. I would try to talk to her about how she mercilessly punished the baby's mother—herself. I would also take up with her how I was felt to be the punitive one, punishing the baby's mother. She was the baby as well, being harmed by me and needing to be rescued from me by the nurses. At this point the patient could be described as having changed to a more PTSD type of presentation. There appears to be a clash in her mind: the part that killed her baby, and knows it, is colliding with the grieving part that experiences the flashbacks and that longs to be an ordinary grieving mother. A central struggle at this time in the therapy was whether she could face up to knowing who she was and what she had done and would therefore be able to change, or whether she preferred to go back to, or remain in, a state of not knowing. In my view, there is a link between these positions in terms of her dangerousness. In the situation of not knowing, she remains a chronic risk to her babies, whether actual ones or symbolic representations of them, and the pathological mother–child dynamic remains intact. In the situation of getting to know herself and being helped to deal with this knowledge, the risk to these babies diminishes, but without treatment or good risk management the risk of dangerousness to herself is increased.

Conclusion

The aim in providing therapy for these patients, as part of the overall treatment, is to attempt to bring about a gradual realization of themselves, of what they have done, and of the kind of mental life they lived before these awful events. These previous mental lives or mental states are the ones to which the patients return when in regressed states. The process of treatment appears to require a complicated and lengthy transition period from not knowing anything about themselves to becoming aware and having to deal with the profoundly traumatic effects of this. The hope is to help them to gain understanding and, optimistically, some change in their internal worlds. This may mean a change from a more pathologically defended, personality-disordered or psychotic presentation to one reminiscent of a PTSD state in which the patient might initially feel more distressed but would have, hopefully, a healthier internal world. This would be one in which thoughts and feelings about what happened and about their predicament in relation to this could be experienced in mind, without the need to get rid of these through the familiar violent acting out. It is a lot to ask from people who suffer triple traumas: first, their unfortunate background histories, second, the discovery that they have a mental disorder, and, third, the trauma of having to deal with the serious violent offences and the impact of these on others and on themselves. I believe that, by helping patients achieve these changes, this psychoanalytic input can contribute a lot to the task of providing the best possible risk containment.

CHAPTER SIX

Containment and countertransference issues in a violent borderline patient

Mary Brownescombe Heller

"*My hole life is filled with worry, dread and stress.*"

Thus Angie wrote to me in a letter sent at the start of her psychotherapy. It soon became evident that this was a hole in herself that felt as if it could never be filled with anything other than interminable dread and anxiety. Whatever else was put into the hole dropped straight through. It could not be contained long enough to be internalized.

In this chapter, I explore several different examples of violent behaviour that have taken place during the therapy of a young woman, in her late twenties, whom I have seen for five years on a once-weekly basis as an NHS patient. "Angie", as I have named her, was diagnosed as severely borderline in terms of personality disorder. She was also of borderline learning disability. The changing nature of these violent incidents reflects how her capacity for

This chapter is based on a paper first presented at a conference in March 1999, run jointly by APP and the "Specialist Psychotherapy Service" (Middlesborough, Teesside).

thought evolved slowly and painfully out of a state of stupefying mindlessness—a state that I so frequently shared. Reflecting on what I experienced in my countertransference helped me to feel less provoked by her behaviour, enabling the creation of a space to think. This has led to an increase in Angie's capacity to tolerate frustration and thus to a diminution in her disruptive behaviour.

To begin with, I give a brief account of two of the most central theoretical concepts in psychoanalytic psychotherapy with border-line patients.

1. *The concept of "containment"*. This grew out of Melanie Klein's original ideas about "a particular form of identification which establishes the prototype of an aggressive object-relation". She termed this psychic process "projective identification" (Klein, 1946, p. 8). Projective identification can be understood as a form of communication in which people may place in another aspects of themselves (feelings, experiences, attributes, internal objects, and thoughts) that, for whatever reason, they cannot bear to recognize are internal to themselves. They are then convinced that these aspects reside in the other person and are not in themselves. The person who has been invested with these unwanted aspects—who now contains them—may be pressurized in some way to act them out, thus unconsciously identifying with what has been projected into them.

Wilfred Bion extended this concept. He suggested that when the young infant experiences something intolerable, like the anxiety and pain of hunger (which to the baby is equated with not surviving—that is, death), he deals with this by projecting it into his mother. The mother's capacity for "reverie" enables her to take inside herself the intolerable anxiety, to bear it sufficiently, to process, moderate, and understand it through her empathic identification with her baby, and then to do whatever is necessary and appropriate to relieve her infant's distress, thus promoting his healthy mental and physical development. In this way she functions as a container of her baby's uncontainable anxieties. Her baby has the experience that what is felt as unbearable and deathly inside himself can be projected into a containing object, where it can be understood, modified, and dealt with. Bion viewed this process as being crucially involved in the capacity to think (Bion,

1967). If the mother (or main caretaker) is unable to undertake this containing function for her baby—because she is depressed, or ill, or in some way absent or overly unresponsive—then the baby is stuck with these intolerable anxieties about his survival. He has no other option than to attempt to rid himself of the overwhelming feelings in increasingly explosive, projectile or fragmented ways. As Bion so graphically puts it: "If the projection is not accepted by the mother the infant feels that its feeling that it is dying is stripped of such meaning as it has. It therefore re-introjects, not a fear of dying made tolerable, but a nameless dread" (1967, p. 116). He goes on to say: "The establishment internally of a projective-identi-fication-rejecting-object means that instead of an understanding object the infant has a wilfully misunderstanding object—with which it is identified" (p. 117).

One of the particular problems for "borderline" individuals would seem to be that they do not have an internalized capacity to tolerate, contain, and understand the anxiety that arises from strong and conflicted feelings and impulses. Thus all they can do is discharge such anxiety through action, either by acting it out themselves or by projecting it into other people, or institutions, so that others not only experience it but may act it out for them—by proxy, as it were. Angie's violent and provocative behaviour in her psychotherapy with me illustrates this problem. She (like so many borderline patients) was particularly skilled at intuiting just which vulnerable aspects of my psyche were most likely to respond to being provoked. It was as if she knew from the start which was the most sensitive button to press in order to get a reaction that would best fit her internal object relationships.

2. *The concept of countertransference.*   This is to do with the feelings, images, sensations, and so on that the psychotherapist experiences in relation to her patient. It is a central concept in current analytic technique. The therapist's mind and body—like Bion's containing mother in her reverie—may be thought of as an instrument that can be finely attuned and responsive to the patient's state of mind. What the patient communicates at an unconscious level can be received and amplified through the medium of the therapist's countertransference. The therapist may find herself being nudged into feeling certain things in relation to her patient, or having

sudden images come into her mind, or behaving in certain ways. These may be very subtle and fleeting, or they may be intense and almost overwhelming. Just as the infant affects the mother, so the patient affects the therapist. When the therapist is able to notice and think about this, then what may emerge with a sudden and surprising clarity is the realization that the patient has been repeating and enacting with the therapist an experience of past problematic relationships, which have never previously been thought about—perhaps because they took place at a very early developmental level. The nature of these relationships can now begin to be understood and thought about at a conscious level by the therapist, so that this understanding can eventually be conveyed to the patient.

"Angie"

Angie was referred to me when all around her seemed to be in a state of utter desperation and disintegration. The referring family doctor wrote that the adoptive parents were being driven mad by Angie's behaviour. Their physical health was suffering, and he feared that the whole family was about to break down. Angie was also in serious danger of losing her part-time job because of her frequent temper outbursts. Reading between the lines of his letter, it sounded as if the GP too was at his wits' end and being driven mad by this turbulent situation.

In order to preserve confidentiality, I shall give only those details of her background as are relevant to an understanding of the parents' and Angie's dilemmas.

The parents' own child, a boy, had died from a congenital condition shortly before his second birthday. They did not want to risk another baby of their own, so they adopted a baby boy within a very few weeks of their son's death. The painful task of mourning their child had been replaced by this precipitate action. Just when their adopted son was coming up for two, the parents decided that they must adopt another baby boy. Again, the adoption process was quickly expedited. A baby boy was ready to be taken home by the couple, when the birth mother decided that she wanted to keep her baby. The couple were persuaded by the adoption agency—

against their better judgement, it would seem—to accept a girl baby. This child, Angie, who was already several months old, had been placed in a children's home almost immediately after birth. Clearly, right from the start there was a catastrophe at the heart of things. There was the tragedy in the minds of the adoptive parents that could not be contained and worked through, but only repeated through these replacement babies. Such a situation has been shown to have serious and long-term effects on the replacement child, since there is inevitably a confusion between the dead and the living child in the minds of the parents (Bourne & Lewis, 1984, 1992; Lewis & Page, 1978). There was also the thoroughly unsatisfactory beginning for Angie, whose own mother could not keep her, who spent several months in the anonymity of a children's home, and who was adopted by parents for whom she was at best a substitute for what they had really wanted. These dilemmas, as well as the confusion as to whether she was the longed-for baby boy whose death could never be mourned or a despised female child who could never replace him would all be likely to have contributed to Angie's learning disability. Valerie Sinason (1992) makes the point that the mental handicap can act as a means of protecting a fragile, narcissistically vulnerable self from the recognition of painful thoughts about the self.

At first Angie's developmental milestones did not give cause for concern, but by the time she reached the age of 6, it was decided that she could not cope with normal school, and she was placed in a school for children with learning difficulties. This was where she stayed for the rest of her schooling. She was unhappy at school and reported being teased and bullied regularly. When she reached puberty, she became increasingly difficult to manage, and by her early twenties she had already taken several quite serious overdoses, in addition to cutting her arms and face at regular intervals. She had been offered counselling and psychology sessions but would so bombard the helper with letters, demands, and telephone calls that they inevitably ended the relationship. Every rejection was followed by storms, tantrums, and more self-harming behaviour. She was seen by a psychiatrist in adult services, who said that she would be more appropriately seen by a learning disability psychiatrist. When this was arranged, the psychiatrist said that since her IQ was borderline, she should be seen in the adult services. Thus the pattern of never being the right one, or what anyone wanted, was inexorably repeated.

She was eventually referred to me following another, even more serious overdose. She had been told by the hospital nursing staff that she was lucky not to have died. My first impression was of a shy teenager, hiding inquisitive eyes behind a curtain of long, dark hair. Angie was initially delighted that she now had somebody she could see on a regular basis, but it did not take long before she was testing me out in every way possible. At first it was in the form of the voices: "The voices say they hate you. They say you've got evil eyes! They say you're a witch. The voices are my friends, they say I'm not to talk to you." These voices continued as a dominating presence in the first two or three years, but gradually Angie was able to tell me how the voices mocked her and laughed at her, how they told her to do dangerous things, and, when she was not aligned with them, how frightened she was of them. I found it helpful to think of these voices in terms of a "destructive narcissistic organization", as described by Rosenfeld (1987). This is a tyrannical internal system which attempts to "overwhelm the libidinal, object-directed, sane part of the self and tries to imprison it" (p. 119). Such a system is at the core of the "negative therapeutic reaction".

Soon though, Angie was shouting at me in her own voice. She would furiously berate me, telling me that I did not care about her, that I had no interest in understanding her, and that I was about to reject her, just like everyone else. When I attempted to suggest that she might think about whether this was really the case, she would look insulted and say, "I'm not crazy!"

"You can't understand what I feel", she would frequently and bitterly complain. "You don't know what it's like not to be wanted. And do you know what I hate most of all? It's that you are getting *paid* to see me!" This clearly was a terrible, mortifying blow. It proved the extent of my treachery, for if I really loved and wanted her, I would be seeing her for free. Whenever I tried to take this up in an understanding way, she would kick her legs about and snarl, "Get lost!" She would find it particularly gratifying to tell me that I was a "rubbish psychologist". "The person who gave *you* a job", she would scathingly taunt, "needs their head examined!" When I tentatively suggested that Angie might have some concern about the effect all these insults and jibes had on me, she responded with incredulity, "But you're a psychologist. You're *supposed* to take what I say!"

I became aware that the aim of this was to communicate Angie's own experience, from an infant, of being unwanted, rubbish, useless, stuffed with projections, and completely the wrong person, yet any attempt on my part to help her understand this was rejected out of hand. As the jibes went on relentlessly, month after month, with very little respite, I began seriously to wonder whether I *was* the right one to be seeing her. I certainly began to think that I had been very foolhardy in taking her on. Under her furious onslaughts, it felt impossible to have any thoughts. It was as much as I could do to hold on to my composure as best I could and not bite back. Yet my capacity to remain reasonably composed in the face of her bullying inflamed her even more. If she could manage to needle me sufficiently for it to show in my voice, she would react triumphantly, "I *knew* you were in a bad mood before I even came in!" What she could not bear was my capacity to remain calm in the face of her provocations. "I *hate* it when you don't fight!" she would frequently complain.

My efforts to talk about the way in which she provoked and bullied me and how we might understand this would lead her to respond vehemently: "But *you're* the one bullying *me*!" Pointing out that this was her projection would lead to the bitter complaint: "Here we go! It's 'get at Angie' time. That's all you ever do!" In this way the blaming and the bullying would oscillate back and forth, leaving me feeling trapped in a paranoid maze with no way out. I began to realize that in my countertransference I was being forced to suffer what it felt like to be the butt of these internal tyrannical figures that Angie called "the voices". I slowly began to recognize that what I had to bear was *her* reality, even though it painfully conflicted with my own views about myself. As far as Angie was concerned, I *was* a malign, evil maternal object rather than a benign one. Any attempt to deny this identification only confirmed her view that I could not bear what she was projecting into me.

Bion, in his seminal paper, "Attacks on Linking" (1967), points out that the therapist's ability to retain a comfortable state of mind provokes overwhelming hatred and envy. Such a state of mind is experienced by the patient as hostile indifference, which has to be attacked and destroyed. For borderline patients this is especially pertinent, for if they feel they have not sufficiently got into their therapist's mind in a needling, provocative, disturbing way, then the delinquent acts, self-harming, and suicide threats are likely to escalate. Yet if they do manage to seriously disable their therapist, then this creates overwhelming guilt and terror, which itself may provoke further violence and suicide attempts. There is a very fine dividing line, too, between being experienced as a therapist who has only a limited capacity to tolerate such a patient's behaviour— thus exacerbating their fury, guilt, and desperation—and colluding with an omnipotent phantasy that the psychotherapist's capacity to bear such onslaughts is infinite. I think, too, that for the border-line patient there is an addictive, manic type of excitement in the whirligig of the violent physical and verbal abuse. This acts as a defence against a deep underlying depression, and this makes the behaviour very difficult to give up.

There were occasions when I would manage to understand something and put it back to Angie in a way that she could take in. Her response would then be a grudging "You're not so stupid as you look!" The problem, though, in taking in anything from me was that it could not remain creatively alive. What I gave her was quickly rejected, well before it had the chance to develop into a viable thought that might sustain her growth and development. In this way, my understanding repeatedly suffered the fate of the infant Angie, who was to remain forever trapped in a system that pronounced her to be bad, stupid, and unwanted.

Some specific examples:
The knife

This came some eight months into the therapy. It was preceded by a newspaper clipping Angie sent to me through the post, describing how a schizophrenic in-patient had suddenly violently attacked and stabbed his occupational therapist, who had died from her injuries. Angie had outlined the story in red pen.

Two or three weeks later, half-way through the session, Angie took something out of her pocket and began to play with it. At first it was not clear what she had in her hand, since she was hiding it from my view, but quite soon I could see that it was a knife: a small but sharp-looking vegetable paring knife. She began to play with it in an increasingly provocative way. She said that she was going to cut herself, "or", she added darkly, "someone else will get it!" She began to dig the point of the knife into her arm. At first, I said mildly that I thought it would be better if she put the knife on the table beside her. She laughed and continued to dig the point into her arm. I suggested that she should give the knife to me, but she looked at me in a mocking, contemptuous way. I found myself feeling distinctly alarmed. The newspaper cutting and the scrawled red pen came into my mind. I said that I was not prepared to continue the session while she was holding this knife. She continued to play with it, looking at me defiantly, as if saying, "I dare you to stop me!" I could think of nothing else to say. All that was in my mind was that if one of us was to survive, it had better be me.

I sat quietly for another minute or two while she continued to "play" with this knife. Then, seizing an opportunity when she was looking away, I leaned forward, took the knife firmly, and pulled it from her grasp. Acting more by instinct than conscious thought, I stood up and walked to my tall cupboard, opened the door, and placed the knife on one of my shelves. By this time I had sufficiently recovered my composure to say coolly to her as I sat down: "In this way, I am containing and keeping safe your murderous impulses."

Angie shouted at me, demanding that I give her back her knife because she wanted to kill herself. But I think that by this time she had conceded defeat. With hindsight, I have wondered whether my thought "it had better be me who is going to survive" related to Angie's very early maternal deprivation. In other words, what was being enacted between us, and what I was picking up in my countertransference, was that in her internal world there was no mother and baby linked together in a relationship, but, rather, a murderous system in which only one could remain alive and the other had to be annihilated.

For some time after this, Angie continued to demand that I should give her back her knife, so that she could kill herself. There are plenty of such knives available, had she really wanted to do this. I think that this was another example of her need to test whether I really was willing to contain her capacity to harm herself and other people. Following the confiscation of this knife, there were no more "cutting" incidents. Occasionally, she would accuse me of *stealing* her knife, saying that I had no right to take away something that belonged to her. My attempts to understand this with her were rejected, so I eventually said that what she was saying was true. I did not have the right to keep this knife, because it did not belong to me. However, I doubted that it belonged to her either, because, I thought, she had taken it from her parents' kitchen. I said that if she wished me to, I would post the knife back to her parents, with a covering letter telling them how it had come into my possession. The knife remains in my cupboard and has not been mentioned for a long time. Even so, there *is* the question as to the ownership of the knife. I suspect that in Angie's mind there is a version of a parental couple who are "at it like knives". It is an exciting version of Klein's "combined parental couple" who are forever locked together in a fighting, sadistic intercourse (Klein, 1961, pp. 118–119). This is how Angie would wish us to be forever joined—and why she hates it when I don't fight. Although I was not conscious of it at the time, my taking the knife into my cupboard "for safe-keeping" was a symbolic enactment of a mother appropriately taking back into her body the father's penis, omnipotently *mis*-appropriated by my patient. Symbolically, therefore, the knife *does* belong to me, as representing the conjugal rights of the parents.

"The slap"

This took place about a year and a half after the start of the psychotherapy. It had been a session in which there had occurred a most welcome respite in her bullying, hectoring manner. After a silence that felt, for once, quite comfortable, Angie told me that she had been looking at a book in my bookcase, which was entitled *Pain*. The author's name—Bond—was also clearly visible on the spine. She said that she had always suffered from a lot of pain. "My feelings hurt, and that is why I am coming to see you", she added. It felt to me that there was a sense of closeness and contact between us.

I said I thought that she was becoming aware that I understood the pain that she experienced, and that knowing this created a bond between us. She flashed me a quick, startled look, before rapidly averting her eyes and returning to her more customary grumpy silences and accusations that I did not care about her or understand what she felt. This continued unremittingly to the end of the session.

When it was time to end, I stood up and followed her to the door, as is my usual custom. Just before going out, she turned to me with a baleful look. Before I was aware of what was happening, she lifted up her right hand and swung it towards me, slapping my face. Even though the slap stung, it was clear to me that she could have hit me a great deal harder but had stopped herself at the last moment. Fortunately, despite my sense of shock and outrage, I was able to retain my composure sufficiently to say to her firmly: "You are *never* to do that again!" She rushed out of the room, leaving me feeling shaken and very upset. It wasn't so much that I felt angry, but more that I felt in need of comfort and holding, like a small child who had just been given a great fright.

I was then left with the question as to what to do about this. The action needed to be understood, but for Angie's sake, as well as my own, it really must not be repeated.

I told Angie when I next saw her that what she had done was an assault and that it had been entered in the "Incident Book". I said that if she were to repeat something like that, I would not be able to go on seeing her, but that it was important for us to understand why she had attacked me in this way. Angie was not willing to say and seemed very reluctant, as well as resentful, at having her attention drawn to what had happened. I had wondered whether the slap had been a physical enactment of her emotional experience when I had told her that it was time to stop. Perhaps she had felt that my announcing this was akin to being slapped, so she was slapping me back in retaliation. This may have been a part cause of her action, but the fuller understanding came a week later.

During that next week, Angie wrote several letters and left a number of telephone messages to say that she had burnt her right hand on her hair-dryer and it was now bandaged and in a sling. Before her session, I was wondering to myself what kind of connection this hair-dryer incident had with the slap. Could it be that she had inflicted this burn on herself as a kind of punishment for what she had done to me? This would suggest a depressive kind of guilt.

Or might it be that she had experienced me as an "evil witch" hair-dryer who had exacted revenge on her for what she had done to me, by burning her hand? This version of events would arise from a more paranoid, persecutory state of mind. When she came in for her session, her bandaged hand and arm in a sling proudly displayed, she told me that what had happened had been that the two wire elements in her hair-dryer had come loose, so that it was not working properly. She had shaken it, and the two wires had touched each other. The hair-dryer had become live and had given her an electric shock. "The two wires aren't supposed to make contact with each other", she explained. She went on to tell me that she'd had such a terrible fright that she had screamed, throwing her hair-dryer across the room. "I was really shocked", she added.

This material was important in helping me understand something fundamental about my patient. What she had experienced as such a shock and so frightening was the fact that she and I, in the "pain" session, had actually made a live contact. What I had not been able to see at the time was that this contact—this bond between us—had been experienced by Angie as deeply and provocatively shocking. It had given her such a fright that all she could do was to evacuate the sense of shock and fright into me through the violent medium of the slap. Psychically, she had accomplished this through the mechanism of projective identification. I had made the unwarranted assumption, when speaking to her about the bond between us, that she could recognize that we were two separate people—or elements—each with their own individual lives, who *could* touch each other, whereas she had the omnipotent phantasy that I was a part of her and under her absolute control. My comment about the bond between us had brought the session alive, but it had threatened too great a loss to her delusional belief system. She could only deal with this threat by ridding herself of it through a violent physical act.

The assassinated prime minister

We were now about three years into the therapy. By this time, Angie had stopped cutting herself and no further overdoses had been taken for at least 18 months—although there were often threats that she would do this. Angie herself never told me of any progress she was making, since she persisted with her belief that the slightest sign of improvement would lead me to end her therapy immediately. Nevertheless, I heard from her doctor that she was now doing reasonably well in her job and was no longer driving her adoptive parents mad. Indeed, most of the time, they all seemed to be getting along quite well together.

In this session, Angie was being even more exhaustingly provocative than usual. I understood this to be because we were coming towards the Christmas break. She had spent the first 20 minutes of the session not looking at me but saying, in such a faint voice I could scarcely hear her, that she could take no more. She said that she had bought some tablets, which she was going to take when she went out of the session. She would not be here next week, because she would be in her coffin. Nobody cared about her. Nobody understood her, nobody was bothered. She was better off dead, because nobody could cope with her. In the end, everyone rejected her. She was so depressed, she was at the end of despair. "But what do you care?" she continued. "You have a life, and I don't. You don't give a stuff about me! It would be better if I was out of everyone's way and in my coffin!"

I found myself alternating between feeling very concerned and worried about her and feeling utterly furious with her. I had it in mind to point out, yet again, how she could so readily get rid of a me who might be able to help her, how she so easily turned me into someone who was not bothered and, as a consequence, felt alone and in despair. I knew from past experience, though, that such comments usually resulted in her accusing me of blaming her and getting at her. I found myself, in my countertransference, feeling that it was impossible to keep any hope alive in the face of this unrelenting system. I began to wonder whether I should be seeing her. Wasn't this therapy just making her worse? Wouldn't it be better if she had another sort of therapy, or saw a different kind of person?

After reflecting on these feelings, I said I thought she was wanting me to know today just how very alone she felt—as if there was no one at all who could help her with these painful feelings—and this left her feeling quite hopeless.

There was a short silence, which felt meaningful. Then Angie told me that she had been watching Yitzhak Rabin's funeral on television. She had some difficulty in saying his name, but it was recognizable. She said that Yitzhak Rabin had been murdered when he had been trying to bring about a peace process, and that this was not right. I agreed with her. I said I thought that *we* were trying to bring about a peace process here, so that she could feel more peaceful inside—particularly with Christmas approaching—but quite often, as we had seen earlier in today's session, something inside her became very angry at the work we were doing together and got rid of it—murdered it—so that it was then difficult for us to continue with the peace talks. I said I thought that she knew that this wasn't right or helpful for her.

At this, she gave me a furious look and very slowly and deliberately opened her handbag. She drew out a bottle of Paracetamol. Laughing, in a taunting way, she began to count out the tablets, talking all the while about how many it would take to kill herself. She said that she would soon be in her coffin, like Yitzhak Rabin. She added that I was to be sure to watch the news on television tonight, and when I saw the funeral of that prime minister, I was to think of her, because that would be her, lying in her coffin.

I was left, as I so often was, feeling speechless and stupid—stupefied, with nothing in my mind that I could either think or say. I thought later, when I had gathered myself together, that my sense of having been silenced and made useless—assassinated, so to speak, for attempting to progress the peace talks—was in direct contrast to my patient's manic, wholesale identification of herself with a world-renowned prime minister, whose death and funeral were being watched on a world-wide scale. This was indeed a triumphalist fantasy. Through projection, she had concretely become this assassinated world leader, dead and lying in state for all the world to see. It was a grandiose identification of herself in the coffin, taking the place of a nation's dead son: a confusion, writ large, with the small boy who had tragically died before her birth and whom in reality she could never replace.

Even so, I felt that in telling me to watch the television in order to see her in her coffin, she was indicating a recognition that I functioned as someone who might be able to contain her despair, someone who might wish to see and understand what she was doing—even if I was helpless to prevent it.

The Scottish postcard

Four years into the therapy, when Angie was away for a week in Scotland, she sent me a "joke" postcard, entitled "The Highland 'Cow'". On the back of the postcard she wrote:

"Here's a card from Scotland to you from me. That bull on this postcard looks angry, as though he's going to attack someone. That bull looks very annoyed, very angry. Maybe someone has provoked that bull. There's a thought."

I think Angie chose the card very carefully, intending me to have a number of thoughts about it—and her. The card depicted a fearsome-looking bull, with evil eyes, ring in nose, huge curving horns, and a twisting tail. Steam came blasting from its nostrils. Behind this monstrous beast was a white-bearded, mild-looking, stereotypical Scotsman, walking towards the "cow" with pail and milking-stool in hand. In the background was a tranquil Scottish scene, with mountains and a little white-painted crofter's cottage. My first thought was that it did not say much for the intelligence of the Scottish Highlander. He definitely seemed confused as to the gender of the animal. The title suggested that this "cow" was in the "high" lands—that is, in a high, manic state. Perhaps the heavy-handed humour was functioning as a defence against the knowledge of our separation and separateness. There also seemed to be something of a teasing comment on the psychotherapy: "There's a thought!" The foreground of the postcard—like the foreground of Angie's psychic state—was dominated by a monster snorting smoke, ready to charge at any moment. Could this be an illustration of how she experienced an internal "destructive narcissistic organization"? The peaceful scene in the background was framed by twin mountain peaks—which looked remarkably like breasts.

Who was the supposed cow that the highlander was hoping would provide milk? Was I to understand that in Angie's mind this snorting beast represented me, along with her deluded hopes of getting anything of value out of me? That was how she was always determined to experience me. Even so, Angie was becoming increasingly aware that she could be a real "cow" at times and had sometimes referred to herself as such. It was not unusual, after a difficult session, for her to telephone the office with the message: "Please tell Mrs Heller I'm sorry I was such a cow in the session today." So the postcard was also Angie's version of the "bullying cow" that at times she knew herself to be.

I think the postcard was also meant to let me know that all separations from me confirmed to Angie that I did not want her. She was the wrong gender. I was only interested in myself and my own boy children. This left her feeling furiously provoked, breathing fire and brimstone like the dragon bull in the picture. It meant that any absence was impossibly provocative. The "twist in the tale" could be said to illustrate how the good relationship with me, portrayed in the background, gets so readily turned into a foreground, monstrous caricature. The bull/cow was another version of the "combined parental couple", forever bullying each other. This time though, the ring through the nose of the monster suggested that some taming might be possible.

If there is one unifying thought from the postcard that might take precedence, perhaps it is that when parents and babies think that all losses can be magically replaced, the confusions that result can lead them into some very dangerous and mad situations.

A different couple

To end with, some extracts from a letter written a few months ago, after a visit to the dentist. Going to the dentist was always a particular difficulty for Angie—so much so that she had to be anaesthetized for even minor treatments. From what she told me, it sounded as if she had to be dragged, kicking and screaming, into the dentist's surgery, as if the unfortunate dentist had become the very personification of the monstrous beast in the postcard. She wrote:

"Dear Mrs Heller, I went to the dentist today and do you know what, I didn't cry. It was like as though yes—I did it—I didn't cry! I was like a nervous wreck, but I thought about you and about what you said to me in our session. You said the dentist was there to help me look after my teeth, like you were there to help me with my feelings . . .

[later in the letter] When I went to bed tonight, I heard the voices inside me again. They were telling me not to believe anything that you

said. I had a row with them. I told them straight this time. I told them that they're lying to me and that I'm not going to believe them any more. Because from now on I know that you are there for me."

Something more contained, more manageable, and more thoughtful was beginning to emerge. There was a relationship that could be experienced as helpful. Her dentist and her psychotherapist could be taken inside her to form a more benign couple who, rather than forever fighting each other, were there to look after her.

The "inside" voices are very powerful and very seductive. They hate any helpful, benign couple, and unlike me, they *are* there all the time for Angie. They do not leave her at the end of every session, as I do. She is attached to them. Even so, there is a hope that their cruelty will continue to moderate, as Angie's own voice becomes stronger.

CHAPTER SEVEN

Risk-taking in the assessment of maternal abilities

Estela V. Welldon

The recognition of the cycle of abuse in young women who become mothers is a painful but crucial issue, especially when court reports are requested as evidence for life-changing decisions regarding the future of mother and baby. In my long professional career and despite my own writings on clinical findings about perverted motherhood (Welldon, 1988), I had been rather skilful in avoiding writing court reports or appearing in court as an expert witness. This easy state of affairs ended some years ago when I was giving a lecture on female abusers and was confronted by a professional colleague about my alleged cowardice in refusing to lend the weight of my clinical experience to assessing parenting abilities. At that point I felt forced to "grow up" before retirement, so I reluctantly agreed to be more cooperative and active in preparing court reports and in giving evidence. I have found it an excruciatingly difficult process in view of the complexity of the decisions concerned.

At times, I have felt immersed in an internal world of agonies and overwhelmed by a tremendous sense of responsibility when confronted with a mother who really loves her baby and believes she is the one who should be the carer but who simultaneously knows that she is incapable of doing so. On one particular occasion I felt so emotionally trapped in that particular situation that I decided to go to an art gallery in an attempt to liberate myself from my painful professional duties. I went to the Giacometti exhibition in London, and I found myself unexpectedly distressed by a sculpture of a woman with hands ready to hold a baby who has become an "invisible object", not only metaphorically but in reality. It reminded me of all the mothers I had seen whose babies had been, or were about to be, taken away. Superficially the woman's face seemed devoid of feelings, although when I looked at it in depth it appeared like a frozen image, conveying unbearable psychic pain. The piece was entitled "Hands holding the void" (the invisible object).

I wondered why on earth, when so many sculptures were on show at the exhibition, my eyes, heart, and senses had taken me to this particular piece, which was so relevant to my work. I realized the impossibility of escaping from the experience of breaking up the most profound bonding—that of mother and baby. I was just too emotionally involved with it to allow myself to have a break. And this is the nature of the type of work. It holds you permanently in its grip.

The close attention, monitoring, and care involved in evaluating maternal abilities place much pressure on the mother and her "satellite" baby. The usual response is to present the "best mothering", the baby representing the good part, both inside and outside the mother's body. However, when the pressure disappears and the mother is left to her own devices without professional help, the incentive to demonstrate the "best mothering" fades away: too often the cycle of abuse is reinstated and an old and familiar sense of being neglected brings back unbearable pain.

In these situations, the mothers' knowledge of their previous emotional inability to bring up babies does not act as a deterrent for future pregnancies. Indeed, the opposite is true: at times the quest for a new pregnancy becomes compulsive. In both body and mind, this repetition represents a triumph over the experience of previous gestations, an omnipotent wish to overcome or even to deny the loss of a previous child through renewed pregnancy. The mourning is intermittently forgotten, and a complex and multiple identification takes place: the mother becomes both the lost baby and the new baby, and the fantasy of "the forever mother", the maternal body endlessly producing new pregnancies, becomes both an illusory and a concrete reality. Freud spoke of repetition as connected with the first great anxiety—that of separation from the protecting mother (1920g). Bronfen (1992) argues that "while the reality principle injures narcissism, it is also through repetition that narcissism asserts itself, tries to antidote the incision of the real by substituting it with images, with narrative, with objects" (p. 31).

This becomes especially poignant when associated with repeated pregnancies in women with a very low sense of self-esteem. Using Freud's *"fort–da"* episode, Bronfen argues powerfully that the maternal body becomes the site of death because it is uniquely connected to the stage prior to life. According to her, any attempt at mastering the maternal body can symbolize being in control of both the forbidden and the impossible, since the maternal body is associated with the death drive, the beginning of life, and the essence of loss and division. This theoretical approach might help us to understand the repeated and constant attacks that women inflict on their own bodies and on their babies (Welldon, 1988). Babies can be seen as fetishes used by the mother as a denial of separation and death; hence the repeated pregnancies may be a doomed attempt to preserve the lost object—that is, her own internal mother.

Green (1972, p. 151) links the pleasure and the reality principles in the "dead mother" construct. The subject, totally unconscious of the identification with the dead mother, is compelled to return to the trauma through repetition, which brings further suffering. He says the identification with the dead mother is the only means to establish a reunion with the mother, but he suggests that instead of real reparation, mimicry is created, which becomes a melancholic reparation.

In a rich and comprehensive study of beating and sado-masochistic fantasies in women, Ethel Person has coined the terms "the body silenced"—the lack of sexual desire—and "the body as the enemy"—producing hypochondriac symptoms (Person & Klar, 1994). I believe that a fitting term for my female patients' specific predicaments could be "the body as the torturer". This would signal the compulsive urges these women experience towards their bodies, unconsciously making them function as the torture tool as they victimize both themselves and their babies. They may present different degrees of dissociation from this, the most severe corresponding to Munchhausen syndrome by proxy. At other times, a partner is unconsciously designated as the torturer.

I shall try to demonstrate with a clinical example the pervasiveness of the cycle of abuse through the maternal body and through the generations in the production of inadequate and inappropriate mothering.

"Ms L"

I was asked to assess Ms L's maternal ability at the time of the birth of her fourth child. I saw her six times in all. Her older three children had been taken away by Social Services at an early age because of domestic violence. This baby was the product of a relationship with a 14-year-old boy, who later denied being the father. The new baby, Kylie, was taken away from her mother at birth and placed with foster parents. Since her birth, Ms L had been allowed three hours' supervised access to her baby three times a week.

From the age of 12, Ms L had experienced sexual abuse by her father, involving masturbation, oral sex, and full intercourse. He used to force her to have sex with him almost every day when her mother was away from home. Ms L was extremely scared of him, and she would frequently wish she were dead. She always felt very different from the rest of the family and said that her father picked on her at all times. This situation got worse when her father bought a small flat, from where he began to operate as a pimp, using her services as a prostitute to older men. She had to perform all sorts of "kinky sex" to which her father would be a witness, and she said it gave him much sexual gratification to see her suffering. Her mother's first reaction when she disclosed this was to beat her, and she later joined her husband in acts of sexual abuse. This escalated even further when he placed advertisements in the local newspapers offering the services of his wife and his daughter for pornography and prostitution.

It seems that both parents were engaged in a sort of "malignant bonding", becoming united "parents" in this cruel and sadistic attack on their daughter, and Ms L had to struggle against deep wishes to kill either herself or her father. She told me that she had spent most of her childhood "opening my legs for different men to make them and my father happy. . . . Where I was fighting it for years, in the end I just gave up fighting. Then I looked on rape as an everyday thing, like housework."

While all this was taking place, she abused alcohol because, according to her, the more drunk she got, the less pain she felt. She said that she had "always been very good at just blocking the worst bits". At school she pretended that everything at home was all right: "I learnt to live in a world where nothing is as it seems. All I have around me is silent fear. I lived with more self-hate as the years of being raped went on. I felt there was something wrong with me." As a teenager she used to cut herself on her arms and her face, sometimes requiring many stitches, which were still visible. These violent attacks on herself progressed to attacks on the outside world.

At 17 she left home together with her mother, hoping they would be able to establish a new, nurturing relationship. This failed bitterly, and after a few months and many quarrels, her mother left her. This disappointment led her to call her father in a compulsive need to continue the abuse. He told her how remorseful he felt about all he had done to her and was able to convince her that she should return home, but as soon as she came back he began to rape her and to beat her even more severely than he had before. He was very angry, not only because she had dared to leave home but also because he blamed her for her mother's leaving.

He would not let her go out of the house, and she felt caged-in, a prisoner. She still remembers vividly the last time her father raped her, because he became more violent than usual and attacked her with a knife. She "saw everything red" and decided to leave home and to report him to the police.

She described the court case against her father as "a big nightmare". "I didn't know what I was to be put through, it was like a knife going through your heart. My dad looked at me and told me: 'I will kill you.' My dad's solicitor was very nasty to me and said I was making it all up and that he had never done anything against me. I started shouting at him, telling him he was sick in the head." Ms L had carefully kept the old newspaper adverts, and on the strength of this evidence her father was sent to prison for rape, prostitution, and incest.

For a while, Ms L's violence turned against authority, but she then began to be promiscuous—a frequent outcome for girls who have been victims of paternal incest.

She started a relationship with Patrick, a well-known offender and drug addict who already had a criminal record, and they both indulged in a lot of drinking and drug abuse.

Patrick became the father of her first three children. At the beginning he was considerate, but he soon began to beat her and to break things in the flat they shared. Soon after she became pregnant, he was sent to prison. After his release she gave birth to a baby boy, Peter, but the violence escalated. She began to experience Patrick as just like her own father but felt very much in love with him. Revealingly, she said: "Things have not changed a lot really because Patrick hits me in front of the kids and does the things my dad used to do to my mum. When Patrick starts beating me up, I feel as if it is my dad beating me up again and that I am the child again. I get very scared because he behaves then like a madman. Every time I tell Patrick that we are finished, he starts acting like a child about to lose his mum, then I feel sorry for him and stay with him."

Her worsening relationship with Patrick did not prevent her from becoming pregnant again. Her many attempts to get rid of Patrick proved to be ineffectual because of her own inconsistency and ambivalence. By this time she had become "addicted" (her own word) to violence and brutalization. The children witnessed the violence, which was eventually reported by neighbours. Ms L said she felt very upset about Social Services taking the two children away because, in her opinion, they had never been hurt. This response revealed her degree of dissociation: she was utterly unaware of the long-term consequences the children would suffer from witnessing their parents' ferocious fights and her own battering at the hands of their father. She felt completely isolated, unable to rely on her brothers and sister who were very angry because she had "sent" their father to prison.

After the court appearance she received some counselling, but she interrupted it because she could not tolerate looking back at old areas of intense pain. She resorted to excessive drinking and to taking overdoses. She said: "Without the drink I would most likely have gone mad. Drinking did save my life in a funny sort of way." Her dissociation was progressing even further. Joseph (1981) describes patients who have to silence psychic pain in a concrete way as the only means of dealing with it. She refers to Bion's conceptualization that people who are so intolerant of pain also fail to "suffer pleasure" (Bion, 1970, p. 9).

A tragedy then revealed Ms L's complete inability to mourn. Her second son, Patrick died in an accident while living with foster parents. He was 18 months old. Surprisingly, she never expressed anger against the authorities over this. On the contrary, she expressed guilty feelings about not having had her little boy living with her at that time. She felt in urgent need of an immediate replacement for him—a pathological mourning process was in full operation. I was amazed when she told me that on reflection her "serious" problems began with the birth of the third baby, John. She was bitterly disappointed because he did not resemble little Patrick at all, and she felt completely detached from John, unable to create any bonding with him. It seemed that this new bereavement had brought alive all her old and apparently dormant episodes of grief. [The attempt to resolve the unmourned loss of a previous child with a replacement baby has been well described by Lewis (1979; Lewis & Page, 1978) and by Etchegoyen (1977).]

Ms L began to live on her own. Perhaps the sense of detached estrangement from her new baby enabled her not only to give up the baby for adoption but also to terminate her relationship with her partner, Patrick, who was found dead from an overdose a few months later. She told me: "My first reaction was a great sense of relief in knowing that I couldn't any longer be addicted to him or be brutalized by him."

There was then a further period of promiscuity, which ended when she decided to seduce Denis, a 14-year-old boy for whom she used to baby-sit. She enticed him with the idea of becoming a proud father, and she soon became pregnant again. According to her, despite his youth Denis was supportive, mature, and kind to her, and both were very happy about the pregnancy, which she said was "planned".

However, what appears to be a new scenario is actually merely the old one turned upside down. Ms L was now cast as the abuser.

She may have anticipated that for once she would be in complete control of a relationship. Instead, as soon as the pregnancy was announced, she again became the victim: Denis's parents took her to court for indecent assault on a minor. She was sentenced to a two-year probation order, which she subsequently breached by approaching Denis through writing letters. During the court case Denis denied being the father of the baby, and she was mocked by him and his parents. She never felt able to acknowledge Denis's cruelty and sadistic behaviour towards her. She defended herself with denial and self-deception, claiming that she was able to have a good and equal relationship with Denis, although his views about becoming a father could not have been taken seriously in any realistic sense. Once more her lack of emotional maturity and her inability to learn from past experiences were in evidence when she was surprised that her new baby girl, Kylie, was taken away from her at birth. She had never imagined that this could happen.

Discussion

One of the most striking features of my six sessions with Ms L was her fixed smile, with which she tried very hard to convince me that she had resolved all her previous problems and was now able to start leading a different kind of life. This smile, and her readiness to laugh at any comment being made, contained an intense denial of her pain and ingrained feelings. The denial and split-off frustration, anger, and hurt could emerge suddenly and unexpectedly, either in acts of self-destruction or in attacks against the outside world. I felt it was impossible to predict whether they might also be directed against her new baby.

Ms L had continually taken unnecessary risks—for example, ending up in jail for eight days while she was pregnant because she had breached the terms of her bail condition by approaching Denis. Her self-destructiveness had continued in a merciless way, with repeated episodes of self-cutting and overdoses.

The suicide attempts were provoked by feelings of anger, despair, isolation, and an extreme inability to trust anyone with these feelings. She protected those around her from her own rage by acting out her sado-masochistic impulses against her own body. It seemed that she could make herself feel better and at peace only by acquiescing to the demands of her sadistic superego.

In her violent relationship with Patrick her attempts to escape were doomed to fail, since she wanted to convince herself that he was a caring, loving person. De Zulueta (1993) describes this pattern in a most vivid and accurate way. She talks of the aftermath of violence in which victim and abuser can come together in a state of calmness. The victim forgives and becomes reconciled with the brutal partner, yearning for the fantasy of "being one again" (p. 186). In this case Ms L was utterly unaware of the way in which the effects of the abuse also extended to their children. She reacted to Patrick's brutal attacks by becoming dissociated, unable to take proper care of herself or her sons. In this way her neglect of the children became a continuation and expansion of her own abuse.

Clashes frequently occur between legal requirements and psychodynamic evaluation. A central issue for the legal system is whether or not these young women are able to place the baby's needs before their own. There may be an idea that a new pregnancy may bring a new start, or that there has been an improvement in the maternal abilities due to other "changes". The problem, as we know, is that repetition is in itself both evidence of a lack of internal change and an obstacle to change in the future.

When I explored Ms L's ideas about what she would like to do in life, she expressed a wish either to be a nurse or to work in an old people's home.

This aspiration, characteristic of those who have suffered continual early abuse, suggests an attempt at reparation for their own feelings of being undeserving, damaged, and ruined for ever. Because of their intense sense of guilt and shame and their own unacknowledged internal needs, they try to provide care for themselves by proxy by projecting onto others whom they consider to be "blameless, vulnerable people". These young women often say that the only thing they want is to keep on having more babies, or else to have a job looking after other children. It is very difficult for them to see the link, to understand that they are wishing to care for children in the way they themselves would have liked ideally to have been cared for. (It is worth noting that this is precisely the kind of young woman who could easily be employed in work with children or the handicapped, with potentially serious consequences.)

Witnessing what appears to be an incipient positive bonding between mother and baby when the mother has had such an extremely poor start in life tends to persuade professionals to "let her have a try" as a reward for apparent improvement. However, there is a real danger that the situation will deteriorate once the novelty of the new baby has worn off. From a psychodynamic point of view, a person with such a traumatized early life history will have to take care of her own needs before she can care for a child. I do not believe, however tempting, that we can break a cycle such as this by offering the mother a baby as reparation. Instead, we should be providing these young women with professional help for the mental and emotional damage they have suffered in their own lives.

CHAPTER EIGHT

The role of violence in perverse psychopathology

Ronald Doctor

In this chapter I discuss violence as an aspect of perversion. The perverse patient operates a paradox: he knows something and does not know it. Two attitudes are held simultaneously and yet are apparently reconciled, and an internal world is thereby created in which reality is distorted and misrepresented. The perversion arises in the attempt' to create this false reconciliation between contradictory ideas that can no longer be kept separate, and it is when the perverse solution proves inadequate to contain the patient's internal conflict that aggression and violence can erupt.

Many people indulge in sexual fantasies that deviate from the accepted norm, and some may put such fantasies into occasional practice, but "sexual deviance" is defined as a persistent and preferred form of perverse sexual behaviour that reflects a global structure involving the individual's whole personality. The psychoanalytic literature generally considers it appropriate to employ the term "perversion" as a diagnostic designation. Although sometimes considered a pejorative term, my colleagues and I find it useful to retain the word "perversion" to indicate a particular sexual practice, and I use it in this chapter.

As early as 1924, Freud drew attention to a state of mind in which one both knows and does not know a thing at the same time (1924b [1923]). Later he was to use the noun *"Verleugnung"*—translated by Strachey as "disavowal"—to describe this non-psychotic form of denial. In 1938 Freud wrote of it as a half-measure in which the disavowal is always supplemented by an acknowledgement: two contrary and independent attitudes arise and result in a splitting of the ego (1940a [1938]). Steiner (1985) has used the term "turning a blind eye" for a defence that is characteristic of what is regarded in psychoanalytic thinking as the "borderline position". Thus a patient who is not psychotic and is fully capable of observing reality can nevertheless misrepresent to himself, and consequently live in, an unreal world of fantasy and illusion. Freud describes disavowal as the blind but seeing eye that is directed not only outwards but inwards, so it is not only the things of the external world that are known and not known but also thoughts and feelings; they are thought and not thought, felt and not felt. In the perversions, disavowal is placed at the centre of the individual's mental life, and it characterizes his whole relationship to the world.

Riesenberg-Malcolm (1988) thinks that perverse patients resist psychic change in order to avoid learning about what they believe to be their irreparably damaged internal objects. Britton (1989) suggests that they also believe that they cannot afford to know the reality of their external objects, which they expect to find devastated or horrifying. In the patient whom I describe, his world is populated by objects that abandon, desert, cast off, disown, reject, renounce, and throw out. These patients do not fly to external reality to escape their minds, nor do they withdraw into an inner world to avoid the fears of the external world. They cannot, because they are terrified of both internal and external reality; instead, they seek refuge in a state of unreality that characterizes all their relationships. This refuge is reinforced by the secret beliefs hidden in perversions—"a domain or world of fantasy kept free from the exigencies of life, like a kind of reservation" (Freud, 1924b [1923]).

The sense of sanctuary, of being in a safe place, invokes an idea of being inside something good. Winnicott (1960) talks about the sense of being held. Bick (1968) equates it with having an enveloping skin that protects and enfolds. She also suggests that a sense of cohesion may be provided for the infant by focusing on a perceptual experience, whether it be a nipple in the mouth or an object of the eye. When sanctuary is lost, patients speak of feeling that they are "falling forever", or as if they exist in a "black hole", or that "there is no floor to the world". Meaning is lost, and there is a sense of internal fragmentation. Often their violence is a reaction to this confusion and incoherence, which Bion (1962b) describes using his concept of "container–contained". The contained gives meaning to the context that contains it, and the container gives shape and secure boundaries to that which it encloses. Freud (1915c) suggested that the human organism aims to exist in a state of psychic homeostasis—that is, the condition of well-being that normally accompanies the harmonious and integrated functioning of all the biological and mental structures. The patients we are considering feel that they need their perversions or misrepresentations to maintain their equilibrium and they often come to treatment when for one reason or another their defences are unable to sustain the status quo. The idea presented here is that, for this type of patient, any threat to psychic homeostasis—whether it be a blow to his self-esteem, an assault on his masculinity, or an external trauma—provokes an aggressive reaction. This concept seems to be very useful in the clinical situation.

In earliest development, intense need for the mother produces a wish to merge with her, but this brings with it an implicit and concomitant loss of the infant's separate existence. This in itself would be a serious threat to psychic homeostasis, and it provokes an intense, aggressive reaction on the part of the ego, aimed at the preservation of the self and the destruction of the mother. Such destruction, however, then threatens the infant with abandonment. In addition, the mother's actual attitudes and behaviour may disturb the psychic homeostasis of the infant and thus provoke further aggression, by negligence or rejection on the one hand or by over-attentiveness and smothering on the other.

When we treat perversion, we come to recognize a particularly important interrelationship of feelings, ideas, and attitudes that stems from this early period. Glasser (1979) calls this the "core complex". One major component of this is a deep-seated and pervasive longing for an intense and most intimate closeness to another person, amounting to a merging, a "state of oneness", a "blissful union". This longed-for state implies complete gratification, with absolute security against any danger of deprivation or obliteration, and an infallible containment of any destructive feelings towards the object. Such longings are, of course, by no means indicative of pathology; on the contrary, they are a component of the most normal and loving desires. However, to the perverse patient they persist pervasively in a primitive form, whereas in normality later developmental stages modify these primitive desires.

For the perverse patient, such merging does not have the character of a temporary state from which he will emerge: he feels that it carries with it a *permanent* loss of self, the disappearance of his existence as a separate independent individual into the object— like being drawn into a black hole in space. There are individual variations depending on the particular vicissitudes of the aggressive and libidinal elements involved: one patient may experience it as a passive merging into the object, another as being engulfed, another as either forcing himself into the object or being intruded into by the object. But in one way or another the ultimate result is a sense of being taken over totally by the object so that the anxiety is of total annihilation. This wish to merge, and the consequent annihilation, almost invariably come into the transference as an intense claustrophobic feeling in the consulting-room, followed by flight, often in the form of missed sessions. But the escape to a safe distance brings with it its own danger—namely, the anxieties consequent on the implicit isolation. Such an isolated state may involve extremely painful affect and may have been a reason for the patient seeking treatment. When a patient envisages closeness and intimacy as annihilating, or separateness and independence as desolate isolation, this indicates the persistence of a primitive level of functioning.

In the perversions, the ego attempts to resolve the vicious circle of the core complex with its attendant conflicts and dangers by the use of sexualization. Aggression may be converted into sadism— that is, sexualized aggression. The immediate consequence of this is the preservation of the mother, who is no longer threatened by total destruction, and the safeguarding of his relationship to her; the intention to destroy is converted into a wish to hurt and control. Sexualization also acts as a binding, organizing force in the internal world, enabling defensive measures to be more effective and providing a greater sense of stability. It is only when this process breaks down that sadism may revert to aggression. When sadism shades into sexual crimes, and then into crimes of violence, the appreciation of the other person as a separate and real object decreases and can become entirely lost.

The other side of sadistic aggression is masochism, in which once again it is sexualization of aggression that prevents destruction. It should be recognized that the masochist gives himself a sense of control: he himself will determine what he will suffer in the role of victim. Studies of the masochist bear out that he will insist on laying down the conditions of the "helpless suffering" most precisely. By means of masochism, it seems indisputably established that he is not attacking the object, which is therefore secured against destruction, and at the same time this averts the danger of abandonment. Clinical experience shows that, even in perversions of an apparently different type, sadomasochism is a ubiquitous underlying feature. Through sexualization, therefore, all the disturbing components of the core complex are dealt with. The aggression no longer threatens destruction and loss, and the dangers of both annihilation and abandonment are apparently averted.

I turn now to some clinical material that illustrates the interrelationship of perversion and violence.

"Mr M"

Mr M was a 34-year-old married man who had had longstanding problems with his aggression and a history of crossdressing, with recently emerging fantasies of a transsexual nature. He was the seventh of nine children from a deprived family. His father, a thief who dealt in stolen goods, was caught by the police and spent a few years in jail while the patient was a child. Mr M felt responsible for his father's arrest, as he had unwittingly helped police to identify a stolen item. He felt that his mother had made him pay dearly for this, imposing on him deprivation, sadistic torturing, and mistreatment. He described her as a "bitch" who never worked but who spent her time in a dirty flat, smoking, drinking, and watching television. She collected money from the children, who went out to work. On one occasion, after the father had been released, the mother suspected that Mr M had not given her all the money. Terrified, he locked himself into the bedroom, and he told me that he could hear his parents talking to one another, saying that they wanted to smash the door down, which they tried unsuccessfully to do.

Mr M had been married three times. He had three children from his first wife, and they lived with their mother. He was very fond of them, and, characteristically, he once said that he would kill anyone who hurt them.

Violence, he said, was his main problem. It would just burst out at the smallest provocation: he could be driving along feeling quite peaceful, but if a car cut in ahead of him, he would instantly be fighting mad. He would chase the car and be ready to assault the driver. He had in fact been charged in the past with assault but had never received a jail sentence. He had no history of delinquency. His greatest concern was over his violence towards his present wife, who had apparently suffered for many years from a severe drinking problem. She was a rather masochistic woman who provoked Mr M and incited him to violence. He had beaten her black and blue, breaking her front teeth and fracturing her jaw. One of his reasons for seeking treatment was his concern that he might end up killing her.

Mr M talked about how his wife, and other people, could trigger his violence by sneering at him or denigrating him, making him feel put down and rejected. Once his violence was triggered, he became entirely uncontrollable, and he would be unable to remember in detail what had happened. His reaction was different when his violence was motivated by revenge. He would then subsequently feel very guilty, because he knew, from his own experience of being on the losing end, how humiliated and hurt one could feel.

The treatment was characterized by his frequently threatening attitude within the sessions. He often used descriptions of his violence in the outside world to intimidate me, allowing him to feel that I was under his thumb. Interestingly, this generally occurred when he felt threatened by me or by my interpretations. He felt like a baby who needed to feed from me, but the underlying anxiety was that I would take advantage of him, torture and tantalize him, in the same way as he felt his mother had done during infancy and childhood. However, despite his intimidating attitude, I never felt that he came close to acting on his violent feelings towards me. He was committed to therapy; he attended for most of the sessions, even if that meant working a shift the previous night. The sessions gave him a sense of containment, and his violent acting out decreased markedly while he was in treatment.

During the therapy, which continued for a year, it emerged that his cross-dressing was, in part, a defence against his violent impulses. When he dressed as a woman, which he did in the privacy of his home, he felt at peace with the world. He experienced a sense of relaxation and fulfilment, free of hatred, and he believed that his violent temper would be eradicated forever if he were to become a woman. Through his cross-dressing he could assume the identity of the mother herself and also become the little girl who would forever be loved and nurtured by her. He was enacting a fantasy of perfect intimacy in a situation that was within his own control—he could not lose his mother, and he was no longer helplessly at the mercy of her sadism.

When assessing risk in violent patients, it is important to be able to recognize the existence of the very particular internal dynamic that constitutes perversion. John Steiner writes of these patients: "The forms of organisation we usually observe tend to function as a kind of compromise and are as much an expression of the destructiveness as a defence against it" (1993, p. 5).

Perverse psychopathology can be understood as being a container for unbearable anxiety, and the perverse patient will usually attempt to convince both himself and the assessor that he is the innocent victim. We need to recognize and acknowledge the sense of helplessness, but we must also be aware of the danger of collusion, by means of which the patient may obtain a gratification through managing to maintain the perverse structure within the therapeutic situation.

CHAPTER NINE

Envy and violence in confused sexuality

Kristian Aleman

T his chapter deals with how personality disorders in the form of destructive narcissism (Rosenfeld, 1971), when combined with dependence upon stimulant-type drugs, can give rise to envy and hate, to violent motives towards inner objects, and sometimes to violent behaviour directed at others.

The discussion is based on the clinical example of a young man who drifted into a state of near breakdown due to his abuse of cocaine, opening the way to fantasies and behaviours that he was unable to contain. His envy and hatred, increasingly directed at women, was expressed through the acting out of sexual fantasies of an anal type.

Beginning with his paper, "Sexuality in the Aetiology of the Neuroses" (1898a), Freud increasingly abandoned his seduction theory and began to examine the role of fantasy. From 1905 he was also concerned with the question of sexual perversions, including the use of the anal opening to sexual ends. He wrote:

> I hope, however, I shall not be accused of partisanship when I assert that people who try to account for this disgust by saying that the organ in question serves the function of excretion and comes in contact with excrement—a thing which is disgusting

in itself—are not much more to the point than hysterical girls who account for their disgust at the male genital by saying that it serves to void urine. [Freud, 1905d, p. 152]

Freud aimed to discuss sexuality in all its variations in a scientific spirit, but there is nevertheless a moral element in his classification of anal intercourse as one of the sexual aberrations. Today the matter tends to be viewed differently. If the two persons involved both regard an occasional act of this sort in positive terms, it is not considered perverse. It is considered to be a perversion, however, if it is viewed as a *necessary part* of the sexual act and is linked with humiliation and sadism. The special clinical phenomenology of perversion, and its theoretical aspects, have been discussed by Joseph (1971) Steiner (1993) and Riesenberg-Malcolm (1999).

"The perfect object": "Dave"

Dave was approximately 20 years old when the therapy began. He had a quite senior job in an IT firm. He had sought help at a treatment home for drug abusers, but without any improvement. Since he was regarded as threatening and was at times violent towards the female staff, he was denied further treatment there. As a last resort, he then sought psychoanalytic help, supported financially by the social welfare services. Dave grew up with an older sister and an older brother in a family that was well established. He described his father, who successfully managed his own firm, as being verbal and having a keen sense of humour, which made him liked by people generally. He described his mother as being more reserved, saying she never became angry but possessed a "keen sense of humanistic morality". In earlier years his mother had sometimes allowed a homeless tramp who was tired and hungry to come into their home, something that did not meet with his father's approval. The children were very young at the time and had no particular views on the matter, but Dave remembers that he never felt able to measure up to the moral virtue his mother possessed.

Dave described how he had sought help for problems in his relations with others and for his escalating drug abuse. His drug career had gradually advanced from sporadic drinking with his friends to drinking bouts every weekend. He began to experiment with cocaine and finally established a regular habit of taking cocaine or sniffing liquid amphetamine 2–4 times a week. Dave's increasing drug abuse was an obvious sign that he was losing control over his feelings. (Somewhat paradoxically, drug abusers may increase their dosage of drugs in a desperate attempt to gain access to physical and psychic sensations as a reminder of their own existence—to feel they are alive rather than dead.) At first Dave continued to succeed at his job despite his use of drugs, but he began occasionally taking sick-leave on Mondays, which disturbed him very much.

The masked patient

When treatment began, the atmosphere that developed could be described as "pleasant and proper". Dave told of various events in his life that were of importance to him, but it was almost as though we were talking about a third person (cf. Joseph, 1975). He might say, "Yes, that's what I did" or "That's how things were", but this did not really seem to come from him or to be directed at me. In my countertransference I felt empty and unemotional, and during the first months of treatment I occasionally felt a lack of involvement. I decided finally to confront him with this, saying: "You report to me things you've experienced, things that could be important to you, but I feel you're somewhere else." His inner defences appeared to become mobilized immediately. He replied, "Well . . . I don't know. . . . I feel I'm here and I don't experience any problems in being with you." I became uncertain as to whether my feelings and thoughts about him had been correct. After the first half-year of treatment, when I continued with such interventions, I began increasingly to experience him as having strong anxieties and powerful feelings. Yet what exactly was Dave himself experiencing? He claimed that he was feeling as he normally did and as he had felt when treatment began.

A sense of intimacy provides energy

In contrast to this, he reported to me after the first Christmas holidays that he had had a remission. Suddenly he seemed much more sensitive, and I felt able to reach him. The interpretation we arrived at was that he felt a sense of loneliness when he was without contact with me and that when alone with his problems he felt vulnerable. Previously, his description of his activities had been rather general: "I usually smoke a joint. Sometimes I snort cocaine. I have a good time with my buddies. . . . Sometimes we bang birds." If I began to approach him with follow-up questions, he slipped out of my hands like a cake of wet soap: "No, nothing special, we simply had a good time . . . there isn't much more to be said." Now, for the first time, he reported in detail what he did at weekends and described his drug taking. He was far more open, and, although he still told me how he liked to have "birds, lots of them", he admitted that he had had difficulties in developing relationships. When I suggested that it might be the case that he preferred men, at first this was immediately negated—he talked of liking one woman, then another, and another, as if to demonstrate that he was something of a Don Juan! However, I continued to explore the possibility that he might feel jealous if a woman was interested in men to whom Dave himself was attracted (cf. Freud, 1911c [1910]). During this period, these interpretations produced neither confirmations nor abrupt denial on his part. He agreed that he could feel jealousy, but this was not elaborated.

The unmasked self

After being in analysis for about a year (during which time much else that was relevant to treatment had been taken up), Dave reported more openly how he enjoyed having sex, "Lying in bed with a woman on the weekend, that's what it's all about." He began to reveal sides of himself in a more honest way, and this led to him gradually becoming unmasked. Dave told of having had two long relationships with women, both lasting about two years. He continued: "Yes . . . it's embarrassing, the whole thing . . . I don't know . . . we broke off because I wanted sex more than they did. . . ." "How do you mean?" I asked. Dave replied, "Yes, what I wanted was . . . simply to go in from behind, you know. Yes . . . it's kind of difficult to explain." In these remarks of his, I detected a desperation in his attempt to avoid what was embarrassing. He would add: "You know . . .", and there was a hope that he and I would be very much alike so he would not need to feel disturbed.

I said: "At the moment you may be having a hard time of it, since on the one hand you may hope I think just as you do, which means you don't need to be embarrassed, but on the other hand I think you'd feel helpless if I thought just as you do, since then I wouldn't be able to help you." This made him feel relieved.

There followed a period of perhaps two or three months when Dave seemed filled with enthusiasm and energy, describing how things were in his relations with these two women and also with later partners. He would defend anal intercourse, saying that it was common among all his friends and young people today generally, and he would declare that the anus is an erotic region. I interpreted this as an attempt to avoid the conflict he felt himself to be in because of his preferences—as though he were saying: "Since everyone does it, I don't want to have to suffer for doing it!" It was not yet a matter of conscious guilt, but there was an unconscious guilt that expressed itself in various ways: drug taking, hypochondriacal symptoms, and various compulsions and fantasies regarding the idea of leading a clean life, such as "simply going out and running through the forest; there you have no need for sex". He often returned to the theme of being a loser if one had long relationships.

Dave told me that he had suggested to both his first and second partners that they have anal sex. It had worked out all right for a while with his first girlfriend, but whenever they had arguments, she always brought up their way of having sex and was angry with him for not understanding that it caused her pain. Showing an almost complete lack of empathy, Dave would ignore this and wait for hostilities to disappear of themselves—unless he lost control, in which case he sometimes hit his girlfriend in the stomach or the thigh. Eventually their relationship broke up after he had viciously attacked her during an argument. She had told one of her girlfriends about Dave's sexual preferences, and she had finally refused to engage in anal intercourse with him any longer. Dave now began to drink more and more with his friends at weekends, isolating himself from relations with women. He also began to read pornographic magazines, watch films that dealt with anal sex, and to go to pornographic clubs in an attempt to inform himself. He said he did not feel good about it, but he seemed unable to hold himself back from activities of this sort. He never had sex with a prostitute, however. He was far too afraid "of being infected with something", and he felt that use of a condom would not protect him.

In his second relationship he did not propose anal sex for some time, but when he eventually made attempts to win her over to this, she said she felt he was perverse and broke off the relationship. Prior to that, during the 18 months they were together, he had fantasized each time they had vaginal intercourse that it was her rectum he was penetrating, and he reported how he tried to have intercourse in positions that would facilitate anal fantasies.

A hermaphroditic inner object together with envy and violence in the transference

After two years of treatment, Dave had a dream:

He was going through a dark forest. He came to a small opening where the sun shone through. As he stood there, he noticed to his surprise that he was a woman with rounded lips, breasts and a vagina. He began caressing his own breasts. Suddenly a large man appeared, a lumberjack, who showed no interest in talking with her/him (i.e. with Dave in the role of a woman) but who approached Dave physically and caressed her/him tenderly, after which they made love to each other.

In his associations, Dave mentioned a friend who was taking drugs (amphetamines) and who sometimes dressed as a woman when he was high. Dave said that he would never consider doing this: "That's not my thing, but the dream must have something to do with me . . . [silence]. I'm not sure what." I suggested that he had an inner wish to gain an understanding of how it felt to be a woman and that the dream allowed him to do just that, giving him breasts and a vagina. "Are you stupid in your head?" Dave shot back. "I'm not a queer, if that's what you think!" I responded by saying: "It was you who used the word 'queer'." Dave became furious: "What's the matter with you?" he shouted, "Are you a queer or a bloody slag yourself?" My rejoinder was to say, "Yes, that's the worst thing you can think of just now, the queer that you wonder whether you are when you enter a woman through her rectum and the 'bloody slag' you degrade her into being." My impression afterwards was that Dave was not in fact a homosexual but, rather, that he saw himself as a combined object—a perfect narcissistic hermaphroditic object. There was also evidence of this in the transference: Dave said: "I can't always make out in my inner feelings whether you're a man or a woman, even though I know what you are. Sometimes it seems as though you're both at the same time. . . . It's strange."

However when I indicated to him what I believed regarding the perfect combined object, he became angry. I suggested that he was envious of the genitals of a woman, something he could not possess. I said: "You also want to be a woman so that you can avoid being dependent on them. The way you avoid the woman's genitals is by having intercourse with her from behind, so that you place her on the same level as yourself—you both have an anus. Although it's an attempt to maintain control over her genitals, it's actually your inner feelings of inadequacy and dependence that you're trying to control." Dave was furious and called me a "bloody slag", saying I felt I was "so perfect".

It seemed that he experienced female sex in general (and perhaps his mother in particular, with her strong humanistic morals) as being perfect, and this threatened him with a painful sense of his own inadequacies. During some of his angry outbursts, he seemed able to produce in his inner world the image of a perfect Dave-object, conceived in a hermaphroditic sense. Yet neither his unconscious symbolic world nor his conscious fantasies sufficed. It appeared that realization of the "perfect" inner state that Dave sought required that he act out sadistically against women through anal sexuality. Through equating the two sexes by means of the anus (a non-genital opening they had in common), he was able to identify with women and incorporate in a distorted way female characteristics into his hermaphroditic inner object.

In Dave's periodically intrusive projective identifications (Meltzer, 1986), I gained insight into what seemed to be the essence of his lack of productivity. For a time it seemed as though he had placed me in his anus, regarding me and all that I said and felt as filth personified. Dave assumed that he knew in advance exactly how I would respond, and he rejected immediately whatever I began to say. I was often unable to finish the sentences; he would interrupt, insist he knew what I was going to say, and complete my sentences with something trivial and one-sided. In her account of her psychoanalytic work with patients of this type, Joseph (1971) suggests that perversion is not simply a defence but also involves an attack on the analyst. I experienced this occurring with Dave on both a conscious and unconscious level through his words and his silence.

Sadism and destruction

The next day Dave reported that when his relations with both these women had been terminated, he had tried out a new drug, cocaine. He had then succeeded in persuading women into one-night stands in order to satisfy his particular sexual desires. He told me that he had occasionally hit them with his fist. He returned to what we had discussed and said that, although he could imagine things being as I had suggested, it was "hard to take, thinking I'm so disturbed that I'm envious of women". He told me it was easy for him to seduce women into satisfying his special wishes, since he was a pleasant and intelligent guy, saying that "women are so foolishly lacking in self-confidence at the start of a relationship that they do anything you want". Nevertheless, it seemed that for the first time he did not feel quite right about his behaviour.

Dave said that a cocaine friend of his had introduced him to a girl who was very young, not yet of age, who did just as he wished in exchange first for cocaine and later for amphetamine. Since Dave had a good income, he could supply her with drugs. After a while he began to be sadistic towards her, attacking her breasts and breaking their agreement that he would be cautious in having anal intercourse with her. He reported that it was as though he did not end up really getting what he wanted. During this session, Dave began to cry (something not at all common for him), describing how she had once begun bleeding profusely from her anus after his attacks against her. He had satisfied his perverse desire and used his sex organ as a weapon for gaining control through penetration.

I suggested that the reality of things had become obvious to him—that he was "only" a man and was of only one sex—so that, whatever he might do in terms of payment, attacks or whatever, he could never gain access to a female character of his own by means of his genitals. We discussed the fact that he had been in tears. One of the feelings was that he had felt acutely conscious of having caused her pain, and that this was something he no longer wanted to do, even if he still felt confused about things.

I will not describe Dave's case further, other than to say that during the remainder of the year our encounters felt less intense and that the attacks against me declined. Also, although the intrusive projective identifications persisted, they became more subdued, and he seemed to be making painful attempts at integration. In the course of analysis, he began to understand his envy of women and his use of force to penetrate them anally so as to gain access to a sort of inner perfection, and these activities had started to become inconsistent with his own ego. He had begun to disengage himself from his desires and to reflect on them, despite the pain that this caused him.

Hypothesis

It would not be true to say that all men who engage in anal intercourse within a heterosexual relationship are expressing latent homosexuality, although this is often a reasonable hypothesis to consider; neither is it true that all homosexual men have anal intercourse. Such activities could be seen, in Freud's (1923e) terms, as expressing a masked negative oedipal constellation—a partiality for the father combined with identification and rivalry with the mother. The idea here is that despite having "decided" to live heterosexually, possibly as a socially acceptable front (something more common in the past than it is now), the man in question still has the opportunity, in his inner world at least, to experience a type of homosexuality through engaging in an act of this sort. Does such an account suffice, however, to explain the aggressive behaviour and compulsion to control shown in the present case?

The roots of Dave's behaviour appear to me to be found in a deep envy of women and of their bodies, leading to an infantile dependence and to a feeling that a woman's body should be conquered and destroyed. The ensuing violence leads to an immediate reduction in anxiety. The unconscious fantasies, envy, desire to control the other person, and the manner of conquest sought would never have led to the behaviour they did without this being activated by drugs. The linking of unconscious fantasies with the use of drugs is decisive here, although the results of such a combination can differ greatly from one drug abuser to another, sometimes producing diametrically opposite results. Some people who take cocaine or amphetamine become completely calm and wish to isolate themselves, whereas the majority, as in Dave's case, become aroused both sexually and in other ways.

The violence can also be noted in the transference to the analyst, since similar envy is aroused in the analytic process. The analyst is, for example, taken to possess qualities that the patient lacks, such as the ability to think more creatively and intimately about the patient's problems than he can himself. What in particular led to confusion on Dave's part, so that he seemed unable at one level to determine whether I was a man or a woman, was, I think, the unconscious ideal that he projected onto me. This led to his fury at my becoming a persecuting object—whether it was the popular, highly verbal, humorous father or the decidedly humanistic and highly moral mother, neither of whom he felt he could measure up to.

Dave's envy of the breast (Klein, 1957) which is filled with nourishment but to which he is unable to have complete and unlimited access, led to hatred and sadism. Regarding the most feminine area of all, the vagina, a narcissist of this type is often afraid of it, not daring to encounter it on either a genital or a sadistic-destructive level, avoiding all confrontations with it. In terms of Dave's life history, one could say that he felt inferior in human terms to his mother; she came to represent women generally, and he thus felt unable to live up to a role of equality in a heterosexual relationship. He was unable to destroy her vagina, to which, I believe, he had a strong desire to relate genitally at a more mature level. The only way he could degrade the female sexual organ was to avoid it by choosing anal intercourse, thus putting his sexual partner on the same inferior level as himself. This amounted to an obliteration of sex differences through imagining that he and she were in the same body, his hermaphroditic inner object omnipotently possessing the characteristics of both sexes. The genitals of both sexes were thus de-emphasized, the anus being focused upon. This recalls Freud's paper "The Infantile Genital Organization" (1923e), in which he describes a boy who denied sex differences, thinking that he had seen girls having a penis. The boy's perception was based in part on anxiety regarding his identity—in Freud's terms, castration anxiety—something that threatened the boy's self-image as a male. According to Freud, such a failure adequately to conceptualize gender identity is common among boys in the phallic phase of development. What was unusual in Dave's case was partly that he failed to maintain the sex barrier as an adult, and partly that he used women to support in a perverse way his omnipotent self-image of having both genitals. This inner image permitted him to avoid being a "loser" who was dependent upon another person, a woman, and also to avoid being subjected to the danger of being rejected or separated.

Conclusion

A narcissist of this sort is often envious of the soft and well-formed body of the woman, developing a wish or a dream of being a person of that sort. Yet this unconscious fantasy is confronted with the reality of being a mere man. Threatened by this and driven by his narcissistic need to be self-sufficient, he retreats to his inner world, where he becomes an ideal object of a combined sort. Our mental and physical sexuality appears strongly linked with our creation of a self-image based on our ability to symbolize. In psychoanalytic treatment, the analyst may be able to help the patient to adopt symbols that can provide insight into his inner world and consolidate his self-image. This can increase the chances of preventing the symbolic and physical boundaries between homosexual and heterosexual intercourse from being pathologically blurred, as they were for Dave. In presenting his case, I have endeavoured to show how this blurring of boundaries functioned as a defence against envy and a sense of dependency and also led to attacks against the persons (women as well as the analyst) who threatened his self-image.

REFERENCES AND BIBLIOGRAPHY

Alanen, Y. O. (1997). *Schizophrenia: Its Origins and Need-Adapted Treatment.* London: Karnac.

Appleby, L. (1997). *Progress Report: National Confidential Inquiry into Suicide and Homicide by People with a Mental Illness.* London: Department of Health.

Balint, M. (1957). *The Doctor, His Patient and the Illness.* London: Tavistock, 1957.

Bick, E. (1968). The experience of the skin in early object relations. *International Journal of Psycho-Analysis, 49*: 484–486.

Bion, W. R. (1957). Differentiation of the psychotic from non-psychotic personalities. In: *Second Thoughts: Selected Papers on Psycho-Analysis* (pp. 43–46). New York: Jason Aronson, 1967.

Bion, W. R. (1962a). –K: Learning from experience. In: *Seven Servants* (pp. 95–99). New York: Jason Aronson, 1977.

Bion, W. R. (1962b). *Learning from Experience.* London: Karnac.

Bion, W. R. (1967). A theory of thinking. In: *Second Thoughts.* London: Karnac, 1984.

Bion, W. R. (1970). *Attention and Interpretation.* London: Karnac.

Bloom-Cooper, L., Grounds, A., Guinan, P., Parker, A., & Taylor, M.

(1996). *The Case of Jason Mitchell: Report of the Independent Panel of Enquiry*. London: Duckworth.

Bourne, S., & Lewis, E. (1984). Pregnancy after stillbirth and neonatal death. *The Lancet, 2*: 31–33.

Bourne, S., & Lewis, E. (1992). *Psychological Aspects of Stillbirth and Neonatal Death: An Annotated Bibliography*. London: Tavistock Clinic.

Britton, R. (1989). Keeping things in mind. In: R. Anderson (Ed.), *Clinical Lectures on Klein and Bion* (pp. 102–113). London: Routledge.

Bronfen, E. (1992). *Over Her Dead Body: Femininity and the Aesthetic*. Manchester: University Press of Manchester.

Buchanan, A. (1999). Risk and dangerousness. *Psychological Medicine, 29*: 465–473.

Buchanan A., & Leese M. (2001). Detention of people with dangerous severe personality disorders: A systematic review. *The Lancet, 358* (December): 1955–1959.

De Zulueta, F. (1993). *From Pain to Violence the Traumatic Roots of Destructiveness*. London: Whurr.

Dolan, M., & Doyle, M. (2000). Violence risk prediction. *British Journal of Psychiatry, 177*: 303–311.

Duggan, C. (Ed.) (1997). Assessing risk in the mentally disordered. *The British Journal of Psychiatry, 170 (Suppl. 32)*.

Etchegoyen, H. (1977). Perversion de transferencia apectos teoricos y tenscos. In: L. Grinberg (Ed.), *Practicas psicoanalitica comparadas en las psicosos* (pp. 55–83). Buenos Aires: Paidos.

Etchegoyen, H. (1978). Some thoughts on transference perversion. *International Journal of Psycho-Analysis, 59*: 45–53.

Etchegoyen, A. (1997). Inhibition of mourning and the replacement child syndrome. In: J. Raphael-Leff & R. J. Perelberg (Eds.), *Female Experience: Three Generations of British Women Psychoanalysts on Work with Women* (pp. 195–218). London: Routledge.

Farnham F., & James, D. (2001). Dangerousness and dangerous law. *The Lancet, 358* (December): 1926.

Foucault, M. (1976). *The Birth of the Clinic*. London: Routledge.

Freud, A. (1936). *The Ego and the Mechanisms of Defence*. London: Hogarth.

Freud, S. (1895d). *Studies on Hysteria*. S.E., 2.

Freud, S. (1896b). Further remarks on the neuro-psychoses of defence. *S.E., 3.*

Freud, S. (1898a). Sexuality in the aetiology of the neuroses. *S.E., 3.*

Freud, S. (1905d). *Three Essays on the Theory of Sexuality. S.E., 7.*

Freud, S. (1910a [1909]). Five lectures on psycho-analysis. *S.E., 11.*

Freud, S. (1911c [1910]). Psychoanalytic notes on an autobiographical account of a case of paranoia (Dementia paranoides). *S.E., 12.*

Freud, S. (1915c). Instincts and their vicissitudes. *S.E., 14.*

Freud, S. (1916–17). *Introductory Lectures on Psychoanalysis. S.E., 15–16.*

Freud, S. (1917e [1915]). Mourning and melancholia. *S.E., 14.*

Freud, S. (1920g). *Beyond the Pleasure Principle. S.E., 18.*

Freud, S. (1923b). *The Ego and the Id. S.E., 19.*

Freud, S. (1923e). The infantile genital organization. *S.E., 19.*

Freud, S. (1924b [1923]). Neurosis and psychosis. *S.E., 19.*

Freud, S. (1940a [1938]). *An Outline of Psychoanalysis. S.E., 23.*

Freud, S. (1950 [1895]). A project for a scientific psychology. *S.E., 1.*

Fromm-Reichmann, F. (1950). *Principle of Intensive Psychotherapy.* Chicago, IL: University of Chicago Press.

Gardner, W., Lidz, C. W., Mulvey, E. P., & Shaw, E. C. (1996). Clinical versus actuarial predictions of violence by patients with mental illnesses. *Journal of Consulting and Clinical Psychology, 64:* 602–609.

Gay, P. (1988). *Freud: A Life for Our Time.* London: W. W. Norton.

Gelder, M., Gath, D., Mayou, R., & Cowen, P. (1998). *Oxford Textbook of Psychiatry* (3rd edition). Oxford: Oxford University Press.

Glasser, M. (1979). Some aspects of the role of aggression in the perversions. In: I. Rosen (Ed.), *Sexual Deviation* (2nd edition, pp. 278–305). Oxford: Oxford University Press.

Glasser, M. (1996). Aggression and sadism in the perversions. In: I. Rosen (Ed.), *Sexual Deviation* (3rd edition, pp. 279–299). Oxford: Oxford University Press.

Glasser, M. (1998). On violence: A preliminary communication. *International Journal of Psycho-Analysis, 79:* 887–902.

Green, A. (1972). *On Private Madness.* London: Rebus Press.

Gunn, J., & Maden, A. (1993). When does a prisoner become a patient? *Criminal Behaviour and Mental Health, 3* (1): 3–8.

Hawton, K., et al. (1998). Deliberate-self harm: Systematic review of psychosocial and pharmacological treatments in preventing repetition. *British Medical Journal, 317:* 441–446.

Hinshelwood, R. (1999). The difficult patient. The role of "scientific psychiatry" in understanding patients with chronic schizophrenia or severe personality disorder. *British Journal of Psychiatry, 174:* 187–190.

Jackson, M. (1997). Introduction. In: Y. O. Alanen, *Schizophrenia: Its Origins and Need-Adapted Treatment* (pp. xvii–xix). London: Karnac.

Jordanova, L. J. (1999). *Nature Displayed: Gender, Science and Medicine, 1760—1820: Essays.* London: Longman.

Joseph, B. (1986). Envy in everyday life. In: E. Bott Spillius & M. Feldman (Eds.), *Psychic Equilibrium and Psychic Change* (pp. 181–191) London: Tavistock/Routledge.

Joseph, B. (1971). A clinical contribution to the analysis of a perversion. In: *Psychic Equilibrium and Psychic Change* (pp. 51–66). London: Routledge, 1989.

Joseph, B. (1975). The patient who is difficult to reach. In: *Psychic Equilibrium and Psychic Change* (pp. 75–87). London: Routledge, 1989.

Joseph, B. (1981). Towards the experiencing of psychic pain. In: *Psychic Equilibrium and Psychic Change* (pp. 88–97). London: Routledge, 1989.

Junginger, J. (1995). Command hallucinations and the prediction of dangerousness *Psychiatric Services, 46:* 911–914.

Kemp, M., & Wallace, M. (2000). *Know Thyself: The Art and Science of the Human Body.* Berkeley, CA: University of California Press.

Klein, M. (1940). Mourning and its relationship to manic-depressive states. In: *Love, Guilt and Reparation and Other Works* (pp. 344–369). London: Hogarth Press, 1975.

Klein, M. (1946). Notes on some schizoid mechanisms. In: *The Writings of Melanie Klein, Vol. 3: Envy, Gratitude and Some Other Works.* London: Hogarth Press, 1975. [Also in: *The Selected Melanie Klein,* ed. by J. Mitchell. Harmondsworth: Penguin, 1986.]

Klein, M. (1957). Envy and gratitude. In: *The Writings of Melanie Klein, Vol. 3: Envy, Gratitude and Some Other Works* (pp. 176–235). London: Hogarth Press, 1975.

Klein, M. (1960). *Our Adult World and Its Roots in Infancy.* London, Tavistock, 1959.

Klein, M. (1961). *Narrative of a Child Analysis* (pp. 118–119). London: Virago, 1989.

Laufer, M., & Laufer, M. E. (1984). Attempted suicide in adolescence: A psychotic episode. In: *Adolescence and Developmental Breakdown. A Psychoanalytic View* (pp. 112–131). New Haven, CT: Yale University Press.

Lewis, E. (1979). Inhibition of mourning by pregnancy: Psychopathology and management. *British Medical Journal, 279*: 27–28.

Lewis, E., & Page, A. (1978). Failure to mourn a stillbirth: An overlooked catastrophe. *British Journal of Medical Psychology, 51*: 237–241.

Lidz, C. W., Mulvey, E. P., & Gardner, W. (1993). The accuracy of prediction of violence to others. *Journal of the American Medical Association, 269*: 1007–1011.

Lorenz, K. (1966). *On Aggression*. New York: Harcourt; London: Methuen.

Lucas, R. N. (1992). The psychotic personality: A psychoanalytic theory and its application in clinical practice. *Psychoanalytic Psychotherapy, 6*: 3–17.

Lucas, R. N. (1994). Puerperal psychosis: Vulnerability and aftermath. *Psychoanalytic Psychotherapy, 8*: 257–272.

Maden, A. (2003). Standardised risk assessments: Why all the fuss? *Psychiatric Bulletin, 27*: 201–204.

Main, T. (1957). The ailment. *British Journal of Medical Psychology, 30*: 129–145.

Meltzer, D. (1986). *Studies in Extended Metapsychology*. London: Clunie Press.

Menzies Lyth, I. (1988). *Containing Anxiety in Institutions*. London: Free Association Books.

Monahan, J. (1993). Limiting therapist exposure to Tarasoff Liability: guidelines for risk containment. *American Psychologist, 48*: 242–250.

Monahan, J., Steadman, H. J., Appelbaum, P. S., et al. (2000). Developing a clinically useful actuarial tool for assessing violence risk. *British Journal of Psychiatry, 176*: 312–319.

Morgan, G., Buckley, C., & Nowers, M. (1998). Face to face with the suicidal. *Advances in Psychiatric Treatment, 4*: 188–196.

Mullen, P. (1984). Mental disorder and dangerousness. *Australian and New Zealand Journal of Psychiatry, 18*: 8–17.

Mullen, P. (1999). Dangerous people with severe personality disorders. *British Medical Journal, 319*: 1146–1147.

Munro, E., & Rumgay, J. (2000). Role of risk assessment in reducing homicides by people with mental illness. *British Journal of Psychiatry 176*: 116–120.

OPD Task Force (2001). *Operational Psychodynamic Diagnostics: Foundations and Manual.* Seattle, Toronto, Göttingen, Bern: Hogrefe & Huber.

Perelberg, J. R. (1999). *The Psychoanalytic Understanding of Violence and Suicide.* The New Library of Psychoanalysis. London: Routledge.

Person, E., & Klar, H. (1994). Establishing trauma: The difficulty in distinguishing between memories and fantasies. *Journal of the American Psychoanalytical Association, 42*: 1055–1081.

Proulx, F., Lesage, A. D., & Grunberg, F. (1997). One hundred inpatient suicides. *British Journal of Psychiatry, 171*: 247–250.

Rawcliffe, C. (2000). *Medicine for the Soul: The Life, Death and Resurrection of an English Medieval Hospital: St Gile's, Norwich c. 1249–1550.* London: Sutton.

Reed, J. (1997). Risk assessment and clinical risk management: The lessons from recent inquiries. *British Journal of Psychiatry, 170 (Suppl. 32)*: 4–7.

Reforming the Mental Health Act (2000). London: Department of Health, Cm 5016–1.

Riesenberg-Malcolm, R. (1988). The mirror: A perverse sexual phantasy in a woman seen as a defense against psychotic breakdown. In: E. Bott Spillius (Ed.), *Melanie Klein Today Vol. 2.* London: Routledge.

Riesenberg-Malcolm, R. (1999). *On Bearing Unbearable States of Mind.* The New Library of Psychoanalysis. London: Routledge.

Rosenfeld, H. (1971). A clinical approach to the psychoanalytic theory of the life and death instincts: An investigation into the aggressive aspects of narcissism. *International Journal of Psycho-Analysis, 52*: 169–178.

Rosenfeld, H. (1987). *Impasse and Interpretation.* New Library of Psychoanalysis. London: Routledge.

Royal College of Psychiatrists (1998). *Management of Imminent Violence. Occasional Paper OP41.* London.

Shepherd, M. (1961). Morbid jealousy: some clinical and social aspects of a psychotic symptom. *Journal of Mental Science, 107*: 687–753.

Sinason, V. (1992). Primary and secondary handicap. In: *Mental Handicap and the Human Condition* (chap. 5). London: Free Association Books.

Snowden, P. (1997). Practical aspects of clinical risk management. *British Journal of Psychiatry, 170 (Suppl. 32):* 32–34.

Sohn, L. (1995). Unprovoked assaults: Making sense of apparently random violence. *International Journal of Psycho-Analysis, 76:* 565–575.

Sohn, L. (1997). Unprovoked assaults: making sense of apparently random violence. In: D. Bell (Ed.), *Reason and Passion: A Celebration of the Work of Hanna Segal.* Tavistock Clinic Series. London: Duckworth.

South Devon Health Care Trust (1995). *The Falling Shadow: One Patient's Mental Health Care, 1978–1993.* London: Duckworth.

Steiner, J. (1985). Turning a blind eye: The cover-up for Oedipus. *International Review of Psycho-Analysis, 63:* 161–172.

Steiner, J. (1987). The interplay between pathological organisations and the paranoid-schizoid and depressive positions. *International Journal of Psycho-Analysis, 68:* 69–80.

Steiner, J. (1993). *Psychic Retreats: Pathological Organizations in Psychotic, Neurotic and Borderline Patients.* The New Library of Psychoanalysis. London: Routledge.

Stengel, E. (1946). *Suicide and Attempted Suicide.* London: Penguin.

Taylor, P. J., & Estroff, S. E. (2003). Schizophrenia and violence. In: S. R. Hirsch & D. Weinberger (Eds.), *Schizophrenia* (pp. 591–612). Oxford: Blackwell.

Thompson, C. (1999). The confidential inquiry comes of age. *British Journal of Psychiatry, 175:* 301–302.

Welldon, E. V. (1988). *Mother, Madonna, Whore: The Idealisation and Denigration of Motherhood.* London: Free Association Books.

Welldon, E. V. (1994). Forensic psychotherapy. In: P. Clarkson & M. Pokorny (Eds.), *The Handbook of Psychotherapy* (pp. 471–493). London: Routledge.

Welldon, E. V. (1999). La ripetizione dell'abuso e dei maltrattamenti da una generazione all'altra. In F. Molfino & C. Zanardi (Eds.), *Sintomi Corpo Femminilita: Dall'isteria alla bulimia.* Bologna: Clueb Cooperativa Libraria Universitaria Editrice.

Welldon, E. V. (2001). Babies as transitional objects . In: B. Kahr (Ed.), *Forensic Psychotherapy and Psychopathology: Winnicottian Perspectives.* London: Karnac.

WHO (1992). *International Classification of Diseases, Tenth Edition* (ICD-10). Geneva: World Health Organization.

Wilkinson, G. (2003). Fare thee well: The editor's last words. *British Journal of Psychiatry, 182*: 465–466.

Winnicott, D. W. (1960). The theory of the parent–infant relationship. *International Journal of Psycho-Analysis, 41*: 585–595.

Yorke, C. (1991). Freud's "On Narcissism": A teaching text. In: J. Sandler et al. (Eds.), *Freud's "On Narcissism": An Introduction* (pp. 35–53). New Haven, CT: Yale University Press.

INDEX